W9-AGD-535

# CLINT EASTWOOD
## Movin' on

*A Star Original*

To Daddy
Love Aaron
xoxxo
X-mas 88

# CLINT EASTWOOD

## Movin' on

Peter Douglas

**A STAR BOOK**

*published by*

W. H. ALLEN

A Star Book
Published in 1975
by W. H. Allen & Co. Ltd.
A division of Howard & Wyndham Ltd.
44 Hill Street, London W1X 8LB

Printed in Great Britain by
Richard Clay (The Chaucer Press), Ltd., Bungay, Suffolk

ISBN 0 352 30083 3

Use is made in this book of the article "A Fistful of Fame: CLINT EAST-WOOD" by DeWitt Bodeen by arrangement with the copyright holders, The Tantivy Press; the article first appeared in the magazine FOCUS ON FILM and is reprinted in "More from Hollywood!'' by DeWitt Bodeen (published 1975 by A. S. Barnes).

# Contents

# Preface

THIS book attempts to trace the professional career of Clint Eastwood, both as a film actor and more recently as a director.

Before starring in the long-running television series "Rawhide," Clint Eastwood struggled for nearly a decade trying to make it into feature films in Hollywood and then became known for his tough roles in a series of Italian-made Westerns, achieving widespread fame in Europe long before Hollywood was aware of its sleeping giant. Since the late 1960s he has made more and better films and lately has turned his hand to directing.

Reviews of Clint Eastwood's films are frequently cited —for three reasons: they were written without the benefit of hindsight; they illustrate that, although not always loved by "trade" reviewers, Eastwood commands a more esoteric following, particularly in England; and reviewers have a fascinating language that is all their own.

My thanks go to the staffs of Universal Studios and of the Academy Library, Hollywood, for their help. My thanks also to the Directors' Guild of America for permission to reproduce from *Action* magazine.

Peter Douglas

# 1

# Early Days

Cᴌɪɴᴛᴏɴ Eastwood was born on May 31, 1930, in San Francisco. America was in the throes of the Depression, and although his parents, Clinton and Ruther Eastwood, were comfortably well-off, there were hard times. One of Eastwood's earliest memories is of having to move around a lot, his father being forced to go where his work took him.

Move around they certainly did, with periods of varying length spent in Oakland, Spokane, Pacific Palisades, Redding, Sacramento, and Seattle. The moves must have been upsetting for the young Clint, who recalls that he attended ten different schools in as many years. "But," he says, "my father used to remind me that you don't get anything for nothing—and I never questioned that."

Clinton Senior, in addition to dealing in stocks and bonds, was a confirmed outdoorsman, a runner, and a sometime football player. Very early on, he took Clint with him on hunting and fishing expeditions into the mountains and forests of California; and during the season, they went skiing.

As a schoolboy, Clint was awkward and shy. He was not brilliant academically and spent a lot of his time in the classroom daydreaming. He also had crushes on a number of schoolgirls, but he reports that he was usually too shy to take them out on dates.

By the time he was fifteen, the family had settled in Oakland, California, where Clint attended Oakland Technical High School. It was here that he was first invited to take part in a school play. He admits that he nearly backed out at the last minute, but he was finally dragged on stage. He says the experience, while a horrifying one at the time, went a long way toward helping him overcome his shyness.

If girls and acting did not particularly interest him, he certainly took an early interest in things mechanical, buying his first car at fifteen. He was legally under the age to take it on the roads, so he had to content himself with practicing on nearby farmland or at the local drag-racing track. The vehicle cost him just fifteen dollars.

At the age of sixteen, he had attained a height of six feet, four inches, and was automatically shoved onto the basketball floor, becoming the school team's mainstay. "There was one guy taller than me," he recalls, "at six-five."

Meanwhile, he was making steady if unspectacular

progress with his studies and was described as a better-than-average B student. However, he continued to resist the efforts of one of his teachers to interest him in more school plays.

When he graduated from high school, he announced to his surprised parents and sister Jean that he wanted to go away for a while on his own. He had already demonstrated his independence, taking newspaper and grocery rounds and Saturday jobs to provide much needed pocket money. He then tried his hand at farming, spending a few weeks baling hay.

It was also at this time that he entered a few local drag-racing competitions. Through this sport, he met two friends, Bob Sturges and Jack McKnight. The three of them made up an awesome trio, and one of their noisy specialities was gate-crashing smart swimming parties. Another escapade was to get together to hitch rides to Mount Lassen in the Sierra Nevada, where the three of them got jobs as forest fire fighters. The trio then split up, the other two men returning home after a few weeks, while Clint moved on to Oregon—to work as a lumber-jack. The pay was good, but there was little chance to spend it—the nearest town being Eugene, several miles from camp.

Evidently Clint still was not sure which way he wanted to go. He has been quoted often as describing himself at the time as a "screw-up," "a loner," "a bum," and his only clear ambition was "to be by myself and earn my own way."

The Korean War caused a temporary setback in his plans; in 1949, just as he was nearing twenty, he was called up and drafted into the army. His first base did not take him far from home—he was sent to Fort Ord, near Carmel on the Monterey Peninsula.

Noting his impressive physique and fine ability to swim, his superiors put him in charge of the swimming pool—with the job of fishing out army rookies who failed the swimming test. It must have been a congenial life with not much to do; Clint even managed to get himself comfortably accommodated in a hut alongside the pool instead of being quartered in the regulation barracks.

Apparently not content to sit around for long periods at a time, Clint then made a move to supplement his modest sixty-seven-dollar-a-month army pay by taking a part-time job outside the base. For the next four months, he worked as a packer loading sackings for the Spreckles Sugar Company in nearby Salinas Valley.

All that extra work could only make him very tired, and he has said that more than once he found himself falling into the pool out of sheer exhaustion. When the army authorities got wind of his extracurricular activities, his part-time job came to an end. However, he quickly found himself reemployed, this time as a bouncer at the NCO club on the base.

Clint recalls one incident in his army career with particular interest—and it is an event that could have deprived the world of his services as an actor permanently. It was the custom of soldiers going on weekend leave to hitch rides on any kind of available service transport. One of Clint's buddies was an air force pilot, and on this particular occasion he offered Clint a flight back to San Francisco—provided he did not mind traveling in the radar compartment situated at the rear of the airplane, a naval bomber.

The journey was not without incident. A few minutes after the plane was airborne, the door of the compartment flew open, and Clint nearly fell out. He managed to lasso the door handle with a strap and pull the door closed, only to find that the catch had broken. He had to hang on to the strap in order to keep the door shut. He tried contacting the pilot over the two-way intercom but found that the instrument was only working one way— he could hear the pilot talking to him, but he could not make himself heard by the pilot. To add to his problems, the compartment was now depressurized and was getting very cold; and Clint found that his oxygen mask was not working.

As if Clint's problems were not bad enough already, the captain called that he was experiencing engine failure and was going to bring the plane down in the shallow waters just off the California coast. Trying to make himself understood over the squawk box, Clint shouted that he had no life jacket or other means of survival, but he failed to make himself understood.

The plane did a belly landing offshore, and Clint leaped out of the rear compartment—landing in the middle of a pool of *jelly fish*! The plane was three miles off the shore near Point Reyes, and Clint had to swim for his life.

"I did not mind the swim, even without a Mae West," he remembers. "What bothered me was hiking five miles in wet clothing to find the nearest highway."

Two other incidents marked his army career at Fort Ord. It was during this period that he first fell in love with the area around Carmel, which many years later became the site for his permanent home.

It was also here that he was spotted by a smart assistant director from Universal-International, who was on location shooting near the base. The assistant brought him to the notice of the director, who had him read a few lines of script—though Eastwood had had no further thoughts about acting since his enforced presence in the school play some seven years before. The director evidently was impressed because he suggested that the young man call on him at Universal after his discharge from the army.

Eastwood left the army a few weeks later and duly called at Universal Studios—only to be told that the man no longer worked there. He apparently gave up the idea of becoming an actor and settled down once more to deciding what to do about a career.

Taking advantage of the benefits of the GI Bill, he had the choice of going to the University of Washington; but instead he elected to go to Los Angeles City College. He enrolled in the business administration course and filled in his spare time by working as a mechanic in a gas station in Hollywood.

It was about this time that Clint started dating Maggie Johnson. He had met her on a blind date at a college dance when he had agreed to make up a foursome. At the end of her studies, Maggie announced that she was returning to Los Angeles (they had met in San Francisco). Clint evidently realized that he was in love with the girl, and some weeks later he decided to follow her.

By the time they started to date again, Clint had set himself up in a small apartment in Beverley Hills, which he managed to get rent-free in return for working as janitor for the whole building. And ten months after his arrival in the movie capital, the couple got married—on December 19, 1953.

The early months of their marriage were by no means easy. Maggie got modeling jobs, and in between she worked as a secretary for an export company. Clint meanwhile was taking on a succession of part-time jobs, apparently with no clear ideas about what he wanted to do.

He still was not thinking seriously about acting, although a couple of friends he had met in the army had gotten themselves jobs at Universal studios—one as a cameraman, the other as a director. They felt that Clint would photograph well and persuaded him to make a silent screen test—"where you stand in front of the camera, scared to death, and gaze into the lens," Clint recalls.

The test shots were viewed by Arthur Lubin and Irving Glasberg. The liked what they saw, and after three weeks of what must have been agonizing suspense, Clint received a telephone call early one morning asking him to come to the studios.

Clint, now twenty-four years old, was offered a standard six-months' contract—at a salary of seventy-five dollars a week—which guaranteed him forty weeks' work a year. The year was 1954. For his seventy-five dollars a week, he was expected to attend the Universal acting school; and along with a group of other contractees, he learned everything about horse riding, falling, performing stunts, ad-libbing, and memorizing lines.

De Witt Bodeen, who was working as a writer at Universal at the time, recalls: "I well remember seeing

Eastwood on the lot. It was hard to miss him. His rangy height, his intense interest in anything to do with film, his wide-smiled friendliness made him stand out, even when he was playing bit parts in Rock Hudson and George Nader films; and they were then the two fair-haired boys at Universal. I didn't see how Eastwood could fail."

Certainly he got the work—some fourteen bit parts, including walk-ons and voices off camera, but also parts in which he had footage and billing.

"They made a lot of cheapies in those days, a lot of B-pictures," Eastwood once explained to Ann Guerin of *Show* (February 1970). "And I'd always play the young lieutenant or the lab technician who came in and said, 'He went that way,' or, 'This happened,' or, 'Doctor, here are the X rays'; and he'd say, 'Get lost, kid'—and that would be the end of it."

The young actor's early films certainly were a mixed bag. He first appeared in a couple of science fiction movies—*Revenge of the Creature* and *Tarantula*. The first was a cheap melodrama about the return of the prehistoric gilled man who first had been seen in an earlier (1954) film, *Creature from the Black Lagoon*. The cast included Brett Halsey, still a long-time friend of the Eastwoods.

*Tarantula* featured a giant spider about to menace the earth. At the film's climax, the spider finally has to be gunned down by the United States Air Force.

Eastwood also turned his hand to comedy in *Francis in the Navy*, one of a series of features about Francis, the talking mule. Not only did he get listed in the credits (he played Jonesey, a sailor), but he was also noticed by the critics. He was variously described as "handsome," "engaging," or simply as "shows promise."

Eastwood was now twenty-four and facing opposition from his parents to his acting career, although it is said that his wife Maggie never once swerved from her allegiance to him. He was still taking his business administration course, as something to fall back on. But Eastwood suffered a serious shock when, after eighteen months at Universal and playing over a dozen bit parts, his contract was abruptly terminated.

In an obvious decision to continue his acting career, Clint moved over to RKO, then owned by the ubiquitous Howard Hughes. For RKO he made a couple of pictures in a lighter vein—*The First Traveling Saleslady* and *Escapade in Japan*.

Although it had a fairly impressive cast that included Ginger Rogers, Barry Nelson, Carol Channing, and James Arness, *The First Traveling Saleslady* never really took off, in spite of what I remember (from seeing it years later on British television) as its quite haunting theme music. The story is about a "women's lib" corset designer of the 1890s who marries the inventor of the horseless carriage. Eastwood had the role of Jack Rice, Carol Channing's beau, and the *Hollywood Reporter* described him as "very attractive"—probably the first and last time that the trade papers have had a good word to say about him.

Eastwood switched periods from the 1890s to the present in *Escapade in Japan*, playing the part of Dumbo, an American pilot. A suspense story shot on location in Japan, the film concerns an American and a Japanese boy who run away together. Although directed by Arthur Lubin (from the *Francis* series), the film failed to register. Hughes was busy unloading the RKO studio set-up, and the film eventually was taken over by Universal for release in America.

These were extremely lean times for the Eastwoods, and friends who knew them during this period recall that the couple suffered real hardship. Clint still was getting small television and film roles, including the part of a motorcycle cop in television's "Highway Patrol," which brought the studio his first fan mail. But even that did not make studio heads sit up and take notice of the young actor.

Even in those days, television was very much a merchandising rather than an entertainment medium. Shows that failed to reach the top ratings at the start of the fall season within a matter of weeks were dropped ruthlessly from the schedules, throwing actors and crews into unemployment.

During 1957–1958, Eastwood supplemented his income with various part-time jobs, including a spell at the Hughes Aircraft factory. He also dug pools for a garden contractor in Hollywood, occasionally working in the backyards of "stars" he has since passed in wealth and popularity. He quit this job after a dispute with the boss. The boss had an argument with Eastwood's coworker and fired him. The story has it that Clint put his shovel aside, explaining that as he'd brought his buddy to work in his truck and the man could not get back home without him, then he too was quitting. The pair walked off the job together.

Meanwhile Eastwood was continuing to pick up a few film roles. He played "the first Saxon" in Universal's costume drama *Lady Godiva*. The film had a strong cast, including Maureen O'Hara and George Nader. Director was again Arthur Lubin.

A few months later, Clint got a small part in a contemporary tear-jerker entitled *Never Say Good-Bye*, the story of a woman suffering from amnesia. The film, directed by Jerry Hopper, had a checkered background, since it was a remake of a screenplay called *This Love of Ours* made some ten years previously, and itself an adaptation of a stage play in Italian (by Luigi Pirandello) roughly translated as "As Before, Better than Before."

The film disappeared without so much as a whimper, and Eastwood returned to cowboy roles for his next couple of pictures. He played a ranch-hand in *Star in the Dust*, an Oscar Brodney screenplay adapted from the novel *Law Man* by Lee Leighton (the novel had won the 1953 Western Writers of America Prize). The cast included Richard Boone and Mamie Van Doren. The film was a neat little tale of one day in the life of a small western town where a killer is due to be hanged at sundown.

In *Ambush at Cimarron Pass*, Clint had his first major part, as Keith Williams. The film is a strong post-Civil War story about two groups of soldiers, some Union and some Confederate, who are forced to band together to outwit the Indians. The low-budget film was shot in ten days by director Jodie Copelan and released by Twentieth-Century Fox. Clint rated an honorable mention in *Variety* (February 12, 1958) for his "fine portrayal."

It is curious to note that Eastwood's last film before starting his seven-year stint in television was, in fact, a major vehicle for another youngster of the day in the shape of Tab Hunter (where are you now?) as Thad Walker. The film, a romance-with-action set in France during the period of World War I, was called *Lafayette Escadrille*—renamed *Hell Bent for Glory* in England, a title probably even more ambiguous than the first.

The film opens as Thad Walker steals a car and, in making his getaway, injures a newsboy. His father, a prominent New England manufacturer, is concerned about the adverse newspaper publicity and quarrels with Thad. Thad then makes his way to France with the idea of joining the Foreign Legion. In Paris, Thad is joined by two high school friends and two other Americans; and since the story takes place during the early part of World War I, they are all eager to help France in the war against Germany.

The friends await their assignments in Lafayette Escadrille, the American Unit of the French Air Corps. One night the youths visit Olga's bar where Thad quickly becomes friendly with Renée Beaulieu. The friends move on to Avord training camp where Thad gets into a fight when a companion tells him that Renée is anybody's friend—at a price. At the same time, he receives a letter from her announcing that she has given up her job as a bar hostess and is working as a conductress on the Paris subway. Thad decides to go AWOL, and visits Renée in Paris. On returning to camp, he gets into another fight—this time with a drill instructor—and is promptly arrested. His friends, however, succeed in setting him free.

Thad heads back to Paris and tries to go through a form of marriage in Renée's apartment, with the concierge acting as a witness. Although he is afraid to leave the apartment, Thad eventually finds his imprisonment intolerable and gets himself a job with Renée's former employer.

The Americans then enter the war. Thad gives himself up and is treated leniently. He is made a sergeant in the U.S. Air Force and distinguishes himself in action. He is finally given leave to go to Paris where he and Renée are married in church.

*Lafayette Escadrille* is interesting on several counts. It gave Eastwood a chance to work under veteran director William Wellman, a man whose eighty or more feature films include such classics as *Beau Geste, The Story of G.I. Joe, Legion of the Condemned, Blood Alley, The President Vanishes, Battleground* (he received an Academy Award nomination in 1949 for best direction for this film), *Good-Bye My Lady,* and *Darby's Rangers*—to name only a few.

The film, shot in Santa Maria, California, starred some fifty young American males and one girl, French actress Etchika Choureau (in the role of Renée). It also introduced three sons of famous actors—Bill Wellman, Jr., son of the director, and at the time a student at Duke University; Jody McCrea; and Dennis Devine, the youngest in the group at seventeen.

Wellman had discovered Etchika Choureau in a French picture. The young woman spoke little or no English, which the director claimed added an air of authenticity to her part.

Playing the role of George Moseley, an air force pilot, Clint Eastwood came up against some old friends again, among them David Janssen and Brett Halsey.

Perhaps that was the only consolation, as the film did little to help him advance his career.

# 2

# On the "Rawhide" Trail

By the middle of 1958, things had just about reached rock bottom in the Eastwood career. Clint's first major film role in *Ambush at Cimarron Pass* had been a flop, and despite one brief appearance on television—as a cop in "Highway Patrol"—there seemed little prospect of getting a break in television.

In the second half of the 1950s, the major Hollywood studios at last were starting to wake up to influences of television on the public. Movie theaters were closing, and there were drastic cutbacks in the production of feature films. The "second feature," for many years a useful standby and source of work for actors both in the United States and Great Britain, was beginning to disappear from movie screens. Audiences lost the habit of paying regular weekly visits to theaters, sitting through two

films, an intermission, trailers, commercials, and shorts
—the whole often making up a three-hour or longer
package.

Simultaneously, audiences were getting more particular about the films they attended—often choosing to
arrive just a couple of minutes before the start of the
feature film, and unwilling to sit through second-rate
filler material. While this trend reflected an upward
surge in audience tastes—and something that must be
applauded—the situation was bound to throw hundreds
of actors out of work and force producers to reassess
budgets. No longer was it possible to embark on big
feature productions with little regard to cost, hanging a
weak script and lavish production onto one star's name—
a process that had almost invariably guaranteed success
in years past.

Actors who did find their way into television tried
desperately to get long-running parts on hit shows. Even
this could prove to be a dangerous solution to solving
one's long-term employment problems. Actors tended to
get typecast and found it hard to break out and get work
in other types of films. Also, shows were ruthlessly tied to
the ratings; if a series started to sag in its second or third
season, it was removed from the screens, regardless of
how much money had been spent on getting it into
production. During his seven years of association with
"Rawhide," Clint Eastwood fell afoul of nearly every one
of these problems. It is worth noting that not many series
survived this long, and actors who fell out of a series after
a year or two invariably found it impossible to get into
another, let alone get work in feature films.

Clint got his role in "Rawhide" through what might be

described as a combination of pure luck and being in the right place at the right time. Clint and Maggie East-wood, still struggling to make ends meet, were paying a purely social call on their long-standing mutual friend, Sonia Chernus, who at the time was working in the story department of CBS television. Sonia had been a friend of Maggie's through their college days and had invited the couple to have lunch with her in the studio canteen—well knowing how much the couple were probably in need of a decent meal.

Sonia had recently been appointed story editor of a big new Western series, and it was well-known studio gossip that there had been problems trying to fill the costar spot under Eric Fleming. Numerous young actors had been tested, but no one had been chosen to play the part of Rowdy Yates, ramrod to trail boss Gil Favor (played by Fleming).

While he was talking to Sonia Chernus in her office, Eastwood was spotted by Robert Sparks, a CBS television executive in charge of all filmed programs. He evidently was struck by what he saw and asked the young man to step into an office to meet Charles Marquis Warren, producer-director of the new show. They explained the "Rawhide" story to Eastwood—a saga of an endless cattle drive—and asked him to read a script for them. East-wood obliged, and then the two men asked him if he would make a test film for them.

Eastwood again agreed, and the test film was shot a few days later. Perhaps worried by his financial problems and ill at ease on the television set, Eastwood forgot his lines. In what was most likely an effort to save face, Clint ad-libbed his way through. Nothing was said, and Clint went home convinced that he had blown the job. He went back to digging foundations for swimming pools.

He must have all but given up hope for the job, despite encouragement from Maggie and from Sonia Chernus. But a week later, he got an early morning telephone call telling him that the part was his. He did another test with Fleming, and the part was confirmed when Marquis Warren saw how well the two reacted to each other.

Meanwhile the rest of the series was being cast, and within a month, the whole unit moved onto location for sixteen weeks. They began preparing stock shots—horses riding this way, horses riding that way, long shots, closeups, and so on—and the actors received lessons from genuine cowboys about how they should act out particular situations. The production was a costly one, set at around $4,000,000. There were problems over the financing, and more than once it appeared that the series might founder. CBS also had difficulties getting it accepted by the networks.

Eventually, in spite of these problems, a decision was made to shoot the first ten episodes. These were done and scarcely in the can before a directive came announcing that the whole series was to be canceled.

This was undoubtedly a severe blow to Eastwood, who returned home to San Francisco with Maggie to spend Christmas with his parents. Clint Eastwood was now thirty, and although his parents' approval of his acting career was still not wholehearted, they did their best to console their son. Eastwood himself was full of doubts—was he going to go back to odd jobs to support himself and Maggie, instead of settling down in some other career outside the movie industry?

Then, like a bolt from the blue, a telegram arrived one

bleak January morning from Sonia Chernus. The financial and network problems finally had been resolved, and "Rawhide" was going to be screened as a replacement for another show that had fallen victim to the ratings. "Rawhide" had its first screening on January 9, 1959.

The steady popularity of "Rawhide" lasted just over seven years. It was a time, I recall, when Western series were extremely popular, and we were entertained on week nights by "Rawhide," "Bonanza" (starring Lorne Greene, Dan Blocker, Michael Landon, and Pernell Roberts), and "Bronco" (starring Ty Hardin).

It is interesting to note that "Bonanza" lasted the longest and is still currently enjoying reruns on many stations. Lorne Greene never really made it into feature films and currently is starring in another television series. Michael Landon appears in U.S. milk commercials. Ty Hardin also did not succeed in feature films, following his cowboy series with the disastrous "Riptide," shot in Australia (and looking like it).

After its initial difficulties, "Rawhide" stayed steadily in the ratings, with one program being very much like another—the cattle were either moving from left to right or from right to left; and occasionally Rowdy took a bath and flexed his muscles, presumably to please the ladies.

Eastwood had a good contract, and the steady flow of work allowed him to buy a small house in Sherman Oaks (which he still owns and, when he is working in Hollywood, occupies). In apparent consciousness of his years of obscurity—and he could look back on ten years of struggling to get the breaks—he caused no problems for CBS, even though there were differences about certain clauses in his contract.

After three years, Eastwood finally blew his top and,

in an interview with Hank Grant of the *Hollywood Reporter* (July 13, 1961), complained that CBS was trying to restrain him from appearing in other shows. "Maybe they figure me as the nice, sheepish guy I portray in the series, but even a worm has to turn sometime," Eastwood declared. "Believe me, I am not bluffing—I am prepared to go on suspension, which means I can't work here. But I've got open features in London and Rome that'll bring me more money in a year than the series has given me in three."

CBS was sufficiently stunned by this outburst to call its star into the office to see if a way could be found to get around this "problem." The upshot of a series of meetings was that Eastwood was thereafter free, during the summer layoff period, to appear as a guest on television chat shows. He also made it known that he was free to appear in feature films during the free months.

No one made any offers of films; but having gained his point, Clint seemed happy enough to use the series to gather together some capital and learn a lot about film making, both in front of and behind the camera. He often joined the second unit to learn all he could about the technique of putting film together. It is at this time that he first got the feeling that he would like to direct.

Television also gave him the opportunity to try things out. If he was not happy to simply settle into the role of Rowdy Yates—a part that brought him a certain notoriety, if nothing else—he could afford to experiment a bit with the character, trying out ideas for different episodes and then dropping them if they did not work out the way he wanted.

"One thing a series affords somebody is great security," he told Ann Guerin. "In a series you know you are going to work every week. And if you try something one week and it doesn't work, you're going to be employed the next week; so it doesn't matter. So you can try anything you want and file all the things that work for you in your brain and discard what doesn't work. It's a great training ground."

By 1961–1962, however, "Rawhide" had taken a dive in the Nielsen ratings, slumping to thirteenth place. Apparently the public was becoming tired of that endless cattle drive to Missouri. The following year the series fell to twenty-second place, and for three seasons languished in the forty-fourth position.

By 1965, CBS was worried and tried to give the series a lift. Eric Fleming was summarily dismissed from the series, and Eastwood took over the lead role as trail boss. But this ploy did not work. To make matters worse, CBS had its own internal problems. James Aubrey had taken over and canceled the series; but when he quit, all the shows he canceled were immediately brought back again.

"Rawhide," however, never picked up, and the series finally was dropped early in 1966. Seventeen out of thirty segments remained to be shot, and after negotiation, CBS paid Eastwood off with a lump sum of $119,000, allowing him to sign for a feature film with Vittorio de Sica.

Eric Fleming, meanwhile, had moved over to MGM studios where he starred in *The Glass Bottom Boat*, a comedy with Doris Day. Then, late in 1966, he drowned accidentally while filming a television pilot in Peru for a series to be called "High Jungle" (produced by MGM television).

# 3

# Sergio Leone
# and the Paella Trilogy

Two years before the "Rawhide" television series finally came to a halt, Clint Eastwood had started to make a name—and not a little money—for himself in feature films, the so-called Spaghetti Westerns.

Once Eastwood had worked out his new agreement with CBS television in 1961, there was no particular rush by producers to turn Rowdy Yates, hero of "Rawhide," into a movie. So it must have been with a mixture of excitement and curiosity that, early in the spring of 1964, Eastwood took a call from his Hollywood agents.

"They asked me," he recalls, "if I was interested in making a picture on the plains of Spain with an Italian director I'd never heard of, who apparently spoke no English. And the salary offered was $15,000! When I picked myself up off the floor after twenty minutes, I

23

asked why I should do a film in Spain when I had 'Rawhide'?"

But the offer was not as ridiculous as it sounded, and Clint took his agents' advice and decided to look at the script sent to him by the unknown Italian, Sergio Leone.

Born in 1926 and the son of another Italian director, Roberto Roberti, Leone had gotten into feature film making soon after the end of the war, usually collaborating on scripts with a historical theme. His credits include writing the screenplay for *Last Days of Pompeii* and (in 1969) directing *Once upon a Time in the West* with Charles Bronson, Henry Fonda, and Jason Robards.

At the time of writing to Eastwood, Leone had gotten together a triumvirate of producers consisting of Jolly Film in Rome, Constantin Film in Munich, and Ocean Film in Madrid. The film—to be called *A Fistful of Dollars*—was indeed to be shot in Spain, with an overall budget of some $200,000. Leone had already offered the leading part to a number of American actors then working in Europe. All had turned him down because of other work commitments, but one of them—Richard Harrison—put forward the name of Clint Eastwood.

For some time the Italians had been turning out rather shoddy Westerns, largely for domestic consumption, and Leone's project had a curious but not entirely untypical script history. Adapting the stock Hollywood good-guys-versus-bad-guys story line, Leone had "borrowed" a Japanese film *Yojimbo* (directed by Akira Kurosawa) about a fourteenth century samurai. The hero of *Yojimbo* paralleled the Western hero in riding into town, dispatching the villains, and riding out again. By carefully manipulating the part of the protagonist, Leone had succeeded in creating a new type of anti-hero who was scornful of law and morality and interested primarily in earning a quick dollar. As a hero, he was difficult to distinguish from the bad guy.

Eastwood evidently was intrigued with the script, and perhaps with thoughts of little more than a free holiday in Europe and some money in his pocket, he agreed to travel to Spain during the coming summer recess.

The rest of the story is classic movie history. With *A Fistful of Dollars*, Eastwood, under Leone's skillful direction, succeeded in creating the now archetypal, scruffy hero—the unshaven, cheroot-smoking Man with No Name.

As the film opens, a lean, hard-eyed, anonymous stranger—the Man with No Name—enters the township of San Miguel on the Mexican border. He is immediately accosted by a band of toughs who chase his mule away in a hail of bullets and warn him to get out of town.

In a nearby cantina, he learns from the owner that the town is controlled by two rival gangs, who are as much interested in killing each other off as they are in selling whiskey and guns to the Indians. One gang is headed by Ramon Rojo (John Wels), the other led by Sheriff John Baxter (W. Lukschy)—and it is Baxter's men who have attacked the Stranger.

The Man with No Name rides into town again, purposely picks a quarrel with the four men, and kills them off one by one. He is then signed on by the Rojo gang as another hired gun.

The Man with No Name then proceeds to stir up the rivalry between the two gangs. After witnessing the Rojos killing off dozens of Mexicans and stealing a shipment of gold, he provokes a battle between the Rojos and the Baxters. The Stranger meanwhile has located the stolen gold but is spotted by Marisol (Marianne Koch), who is being held prisoner on the Rojo hacienda. He escapes with her and then hands her over to the Baxters, who plan to exchange her for their son who is being held prisoner by the Rojos.

The Stranger further complicates matters between the two rival gangs until, finally, Rojo sets his men on the Baxters, as he thinks they are hiding the Man with No Name.

But the Stranger is hiding outside town in an abandoned mine. He returns to town and, in a furious gunfight, kills off every member of the Rojo gang.

Then, enigmatic as ever, he rides out of town on a mule.

The film was completed according to schedule during the summer of 1961, and Eastwood returned to Hollywood and "Rawhide," thinking that that was the last he would hear of it.

The film was initially released in Europe, and by the end of 1964, it had virtually started an Eastwood cult. In Italy the film had taken in more money at the box office than *Mary Poppins* and *My Fair Lady* (nearly $7 million by October 1967), and Eastwood was becoming known as "the fastest draw in Italian movies." Vittorio de Sica proclaimed him "the new Gary Cooper" (curiously, in his early days at Universal Studios the secretaries had nicknamed him Coop), and in South America Eastwood had become known as "the gunman with the green eyes."

Word of all this reached Clint Eastwood virtually by

accident, shortly after the release of the film. James
Bacon, a columnist on the *New York Herald Examiner*,
happened to be in Paris where he conducted an interview
with Sophia Loren. The Italian film came up in conversation, and Miss Loren asked the journalist who was this
unknown American actor who was quickly becoming the
biggest box-office draw in Italy—bigger even than
Marcello Mastroianni. In due course, Bacon relayed the
information he had gleaned to Clint Eastwood. (Bacon's
report was to cost Leone quite a lot of cash.)

Because of legal problems connected with its similarity
to *Yojimbo*, *A Fistful of Dollars* was not released in the
United States until 1967. When it finally made its
appearance in February of that year, the reviewers raised
howls of protest.

Bosley Crowther, writing in the *New York Times*, said
that the film "over-indulges the cliché elements of the
Western formula to a point where it takes on the aspect
of deliberately high-blown cowboy camp" and went on
to complain about the excessive violence in the film. But
his most scathing criticism is reserved for the use of an
anti-hero whose lack of a moral code "is a violation of the
happy, romantic myth that has kept this type of picture
popular through the years."

*Time* magazine (October 2, 1967) was even more
scathing in its comments, suggesting that Clint Eastwood
"was not paid by the word, for he hardly talks at all" and
concluding: "Like the villains, it was shot in Spain; a pity
it was not buried there."

However, the *Los Angeles Times* (January 19, 1967)
suggested that the film should not be taken too seriously

and urged viewers to watch it "to study the evolution undergone by a Yankee Western after it has been processed by an Italian director."

(It is interesting to note that, undaunted by the mounting crescendo of protest, United Artists quickly decided to rush out the two sequels in 1967 and 1968.)

By the spring of 1965, Sergio Leone had been making fresh overtures to Clint Eastwood. This time he had an even more impressive package to offer the American actor—a budget of $600,000; a second American star's name, Lee Van Cleef; and a surprise newcomer, a young Italian actor, Gian Maria Volonte. After protracted negotiations, during which Eastwood undoubtedly reminded the Italian of his drawing power in Europe, he agreed to travel once again to Spain during the summer —for a salary of $50,000 plus a percentage of the European box-office gross. The film was *For a Few Dollars More*.

The story is set in the old Southwest in the period shortly after the Civil War. Two bounty hunters are on the trail of a robber: one of them is the Man with No Name, a cold-eyed, slim young man, wearing a poncho; the other is suave, frock-coated Colonel Mortimer, lately of the Confederate Army (played by Lee Van Cleef). Their quarry is Indio (played by Volonte), who has recently escaped from prison and who, many years before, had been responsible for the death of Mortimer's sister. There is a price of $10,000 on his head, plus rewards for the capture of his henchmen.

Untypically, the two hunters agree to join forces and split the rewards. They move toward El Paso, where the

largest and richest bank is located, as they feel sure that
Indio will make it his target.

In order to gain Indio's confidence, the Stranger helps
Indio's best friend escape from jail. The Man with No
Name is then made a member of the gang: his job—with
three companions—will be to create a distraction by
robbing a small bank in a nearby town, leaving the field
clear for an attack on the bank in El Paso.

Instead, the Stranger kills his three henchmen. A posse
rides out of El Paso, and Indio and his men attack the
bank—they are so swift and efficient that the bounty
hunters cannot stop them.

At the Colonel's suggestion, the Stranger rejoins Indio
and makes an excuse for the disappearance of the three
men. The Colonel has suggested that they move north,
but—in an attempt at double-cross—the Stranger persuades Indio to move south. The Colonel has anticipated
this move and is waiting for them.

The Colonel and the Man with No Name decide to join
forces again and try to double-cross Indio by making off
with the contents of a safe he has helped them rob. Indio,
however, catches up with them—but not before they
have hidden the money. He has them tortured, but they
refuse to reveal the hiding place.

Indio then tries another plan. He has the Stranger and
the Colonel set free and then sends his gang out to
find them. A wild fight follows, during which the
Colonel and the Man with No Name kill off all the gang
members. But Indio is still alive, and the Colonel sets out
to avenge his sister's death.

His personal score is settled, but the Colonel wishes to
have no part of the reward money. Instead, the Man

with No Name is left to return the stolen cash, deliver the bodies, and collect the bounty money.

For the first time Clint Eastwood was up against an actor even more sullen and mean-eyed than himself! Even at this time, Lee Van Cleef had chalked up an impressive professional record. He was born in Somerville, New Jersey, in January 1925. He joined the navy at the age of seventeen and served for the duration of the war. After his discharge, he worked in summer camps and performed odd jobs before starting to appear in little theater groups. Armed with this slight acting experience, he moved to Hollywood, where he made his screen debut in 1952 in *High Noon*. This was followed by a whole string of adventure and Western films, including *The Big Combo*, *A Man Alone*, *Tribute to a Bad Man*, *The Tin Star*, *The Young Lions*, *Ride Lonesome*, and many others.

By contrast, Gian Maria Volonte came to the film from the classical stage. From the age of twenty-two, he had toured Italy with an "actors' caravan," playing Shakespearean and French classics and working at everything from stagehand to director. Famous for his fiery temperament, he was obliged to spend three years in professional wilderness when he was banned from appearing on Italian radio and television after walking off the set following an argument with a director about proposed changes in a telecast of, fittingly, Dostoevsky's *Crime and Punishment*. Sergio Leone's faith in the young actor was amply justified when Volonte went on to appear in 1970 in *Investigation of a Citizen above Suspicion*, a film that became a classic.

*For a Few Dollars More* was shot on location near

Madrid and also outside Almería in southern Spain, helping to further establish the region as something of a minor European film capital. Further exteriors were shot in Rome, on a specially constructed village set, while the interiors were completed at the Cinecitta studios.

Accustomed as he was to Hollywood methods, Clint Eastwood must have been somewhat baffled by the continual improvisation by the authors, costume designers, and director, though doubtless he took careful note of everything that went on and stored it up for eventual use when he got around to directing his own pictures. A company that two months earlier had been turning out chariots and tanks now turned its work force over to the production of stagecoaches and buckboards. Pompeii, the shoemakers famous for their Roman sandals, switched their entire production line and within a week had made leather boots for the entire cast. And Jaeger, a firm of Milanese craftsmen, sent down a full collection of Winchesters and Colt 45s that really worked. The film somehow got made in the midst of all this activity, thanks in no small part to the energy and resourcefulness of the Italian director.

Critical reaction to *For a Few Dollars More* was once again negative. *Cue* magazine (July 15, 1967) condemned the film as "a big nothing. The acting is a bore, the plot second-rate." Stating that "the only basic 'appeal' is the endless killing and efforts to glory in the sadistic," *Cue* asked the rhetorical question, "This is entertainment?"

Although Richard Davis, writing for *Films and Filming* (London, March 1968), also condemned "these bastardized Westerns," he did find that "a certain tongue-in-cheek satyrical air sweeps through [the film] like the sun through clouds." Davis also reserved a note of praise for Lee Van Cleef's development as an actor. Unfortunately, Clint Eastwood only merited the note that he "strides through the proceedings with one grimly set expression."

*Time* magazine (July 21, 1967), noting that the film's predecessor had as its "sole distinction" the introduction of Clint Eastwood, stated that "as before acting is forbidden and histrionics are kept to a contest of who can give his lip the tightest curl and who can give his eyes the narrowest squint."

While Clint Eastwood and his wife Maggie were in Rome, they met the Italian director Vittorio de Sica, the man who a year earlier had hailed Eastwood as the new Gary Cooper. The outcome of their meeting was that de Sica asked Clint to appear in a sequence of the *The Witches* (*Le Streghe*), a five part anthology in which each segment starred Silvana Mangano, wife of co-director Dino de Laurentiis.

Miss Mangano was making her return to films after several years' absence, and the short-episode compilation was a favorite ploy among Italian film makers for showcasing talent. However, the form has never really found an audience in America. Indeed, *Variety* (March 19, 1969) issued this statement on *The Witches*: "The film starts a steady and fatal final slump from the elegant and claustrophobic first Visconti sketch to the dismal, pointless De Sica bit at the end. It is just possible that sequence pics that evolved out of the post-war neo-realism school have nearly reached the age of an honorable burial."

Eastwood starred in the fifth and final segment playing the husband of Giovanna (played by Miss Mangano), in a sequence entitled *A Night Like Any Other*. The series had a high budget, and the production was lavish; besides de Sica and Visconti, other segments were directed by Pier Paolo Pasolini and other well-known Italian directors. *A Night Like Any Other* in no way stands up to comparison with Visconti's later work (*Rocco and His Brothers, Death in Venice*) nor that of Pasolini (*Theorem, Canterbury Tales, Roma*).

After completing *The Witches* in the autumn of 1965, Clint Eastwood returned to Hollywood to face the squabbling over the end of the "Rawhide" series. A settlement was reached by the following February, by which time negotiations were already under way for a third Leone production.

This time the budget was even more impressive—at $1,200,000, out of which was to be paid Eastwood's salary of $250,000 plus a share of the gross (probably around ten per cent), based on Western hemisphere profits. In addition to Eastwood and Lee Van Cleef, Leone had lined up yet another well-known American baddie, Eli Wallach, perhaps the meanest of them all.

Wallach's professional career had shown some remarkable ups and downs. He was born in Brooklyn, New York, in 1915, and after some early schooling at Erasmus Hall, he went on to the University of Texas to gain a B.A. in education. He followed this with a master's degree at City College of New York and was meanwhile appearing in small parts at the university theater.

When World War II intervened, he was drafted into

the army as a private in 1941. He saw service in Europe and the United States before his discharge as a captain four years later. He decided to return to acting and, after a number of attempts, made his Broadway debut in an antiwar play called *Skydrift*. Three years later, he appeared with Katharine Cornell in *Antony and Cleopatra* and then had a two-year run in the successful *Mister Roberts*.

His entry into films had been sensational in *Baby Doll* (1956), the Elia Kazan film that became an instant if controversial success. His preparation for the role of Tuco, the ruthless adventurer in Leone's latest Italo-Western, was completed with excellent performances in *The Magnificent Seven* and *How the West Was Won*.

And thus *The Good, the Bad and the Ugly* was born, another tale of an uneasy partnership between two men basically out to look after themselves. Set in the American Southwest during the Civil War, the story concerns three dangerous men who are searching for a cashbox containing $200,000 that has been stolen and hidden. The three are the Man with No Name; Tuco, a Mexican gunman; and a criminal called Setenza.

The first two have formed an uneasy alliance: Tuco has a price on his head and allows the Stranger to turn him over to the law in order to collect the ransom. As Tuco is about to be hanged, the Stranger levels his rifle and shoots, cutting the rope. The two then ride off, ready to repeat the trick in another town.

Setenza meanwhile is pursuing the search on his own and finds that Bill Carson—the man who knows the location of the cashbox—has joined the Confederate Army in Santa Fe.

Tuco and the Stranger continue to fool the authorities —until the plan fails when the Stranger misfires. Tuco then decides to betray his companion and collect the reward of $4,000 on *his* head. Arriving in Santa Fe, the Stranger is set on by Tuco and his accomplices. He manages to kill the four men but is captured by Tuco, who drags him off to the desert.

There they encounter a wagon loaded with dead and dying Confederate soldiers. One of them, barely alive, begs for water. As Tuco prepares to shoot him, the soldier offers him $200,000. Tuco rushes off to find water but returns to find that the man, Carson, has died—but not before confiding to the Stranger the location of the cashbox. Tuco is now faced with the prospect of keeping the Stranger alive and friendly.

The two allies dress up in Confederate uniforms and set out to find the money. Along the way, they are captured by Union soldiers and brought before Setenza, now a sergeant. Tuco introduces himself as Carson—and is promptly tortured until he reveals the whereabouts of the money.

Setenza and the Stranger make a deal to share the money, and all three set off once again—their allegiances changing as circumstances alter. Finally the three reach Sad Hill where the money is buried in one of the graves. Setenza gets killed in an argument, leaving only Tuco and the Man with No Name to fight it out.

Since the locale of the story was Mexico, Leone decided to film again in the southern Spanish province of Almería and amid the stark rolling hill scenery around Burgos to the north.

By the end of 1966, Clint Eastwood had completed the

"paella trilogy." Although none of the films had yet been shown in the United States, he was well on his way to becoming a rich man. It was not until 1967 that the first two *Dollar* films were released by United Artists and were being shown in the United States. A year later, *The Good, the Bad and the Ugly* was being exhibited, with theater owners often showing two or three of the films together in a massive Eastwood double or triple bill.

Upon its release, *The Good, the Bad and the Ugly* fell victim to the same negative critical reaction that had been given to the two previous *Dollar* movies. Although *Time* magazine (February 9, 1968) praised Leone's expert camera-work, it could not resist condemning "the wooden acting . . . Leone's addiction to the cramped values . . . of the comic strip," as well as what it described as Leone's "insatiable appetite for beatings, maulings, and mutilations, complete with close-ups of mashed-in faces and death rattle sound effects." Clint Eastwood's acting was described as "consistently awful," but even *Time* had to admit that he nevertheless was raking in the money.

There were, however, those critics who found *The Good, the Bad and the Ugly* to have certain merit. As Raymond Durgnat, writing for *Films and Filming* (London, November 1968), pointed out at the end of his review: " . . . does historical fact matter if the result tickles one's imagination? The Western myth has never stood still in the past. Why shouldn't it evolve again?" Durgnat even went so far as to state that "the events are interesting in themselves, being original, spectacular, and outrageous."

Hollywood executives by this time were starting to wake up to the fact that they possibly had a star on their hands—how could they have overlooked him during all those years of "Rawhide"? The result was a number of offers for film projects. The first of them was a carbon-copy American version of an Italian Western titled *Hang 'Em High* (United Artists). This was quickly followed by an action-adventure film, *Coogan's Bluff* (Universal), and an MGM war epic, *Where Eagles Dare*, in which Clint Eastwood was to costar alongside Richard Burton.

The Italians had become a little upset that the man they had helped create apparently was now turning his back on them. A couple of small Italian production companies tried to cash in on the Eastwood aura in Europe by purchasing "Rawhide" segments (from CBS in the United States) and releasing them as the latest Clint Eastwood feature film. To the end, "Rawhide" had been shot in black and white, as there were no stock shots available of the cattle drove, so crude coloring had to be added. The segments (directed by two different directors and in no way related) were strung together and released either as *The Magnificent Stranger* (Jolly Film) or *El Gringhero* (Lucas).

Clint Eastwood was obliged to take advertising space in the trade papers to publish a disclaimer, and this was quickly followed by threatening noises and lawsuits from the U.A. lawyers. Eventually the compilations were dropped.

The year 1968 also witnessed two births in the Eastwood family: the arrival of a son, Kyle Clinton, who was born in Santa Monica on May 19; and the foundation of Eastwood's own Malpaso Company by his then business manager, the late Irving Leonard—a move that was to have considerable influence on his subsequent work in films.

# 4

# The American-Made
# Italian-Style Westerns

*Hang 'Em High* was the first American-made Western in the Italian tradition—dubbed by some observers as "the supreme compliment" to Sergio Leone and his compatriots. The film was handsomely budgeted and cast, a joint production with Leonard Freeman and Eastwood's newly formed Malpaso Company.

The script, written by Leonard Freeman and Mel Goldberg, is a story set in the Oklahoma territory during the 1870s. The protagonist, Jed Cooper (played by Eastwood), is barely saved from hanging and, in spite of advice from Judge Adam Fenton, swears he will have his revenge. Fenton appoints Jed deputy marshal—a task he carries out with ruthless efficiency, bringing numerous criminals (alive or dead) to Fort Grant's bar of justice.

Off duty, Jed becomes interested in Rachel, the owner

39

of the local store, and in Jennifer, pride of the local brothel.

His attention distracted while watching a hanging, Jed is shot down by Captain Wilson, leader of the gang that intended to lynch him. Wilson and other members of the gang manage to get away.

Rachel nurses Jed back to health, and on a picnic outing, he tries to make love to her. His attempt is thwarted as he learns that she was once savagely raped by two bandits who still have never been caught.

When he has completely recovered, Jed starts again in pursuit of the lynch gang. Two of the gang members desert Wilson, leaving two remaining. Jed trails them to Wilson's ranch house. Both try to jump him, but they are stabbed or gunned down. Alone now, Jed enters the deserted, silent house—to find Wilson hanging by the neck from one of the rafters.

Director Ted Post came to the film from television, from which he had an impressive list of credits, including one feature film—*The Legend of Tom Dooley*.

Principal photography for the film took place in New Mexico, Southern California, and the back lot at MGM in Hollywood. Some of the most outstanding scenes were shot in and around the White Sands National Monument in New Mexico (close to the site of the first atomic explosion back in 1945). The unusual terrain consists of some 200,000 acres of gypsum deposits that form constantly shifting dunes up to fifty feet high but turn rock hard in the fierce heat.

The unit based itself at the Ramada Inn at Las Cruces, within comfortable reach of the Rio Grande, which is seen in the film's opening sequences. They were also close to the Organ Mountains, which were filmed for sequences requiring rocky terrain. In the sequence in which Eastwood and costar Inger Stevens go off for a picnic, the company set up for a day at the Albertson Ranch in the Conejo Valley, some forty miles from Hollywood. The township of Fort Grant was recreated on Lot Three at the MGM Studios in Hollywood and was used as the site of the largest crowd sequence to be shot in the film capital since the Atlanta depot scene in *Gone with the Wind* back in 1939.

In a no-expense-spared jab at the new Italo-Western genre, United Artists lined up a strong cast. In addition to paying out Eastwood's not inconsiderable salary (not yet up to the $1,000,000 he later commanded but rising steadily), large salaries would go to the rest of the cast, including award-winner Ed Begley, Pat Hingle, and Inger Stevens.

Begley was a veteran of *Sweet Bird of Youth* (for which he won an Academy Award), an adaptation of the Tennessee Williams play, and *Billion Dollar Brain*, which he shot in England with Michael Caine. Begley tackled the key role of Captain Wilson, a wealthy ranch owner who is forced by events to become the leader of a lynch mob.

Pat Hingle came from the Broadway stage where, in 1953, he made his debut in *End as a Man*. He had over 150 film and television roles to his credit before coming to public notice in MGM's *Sol Madrid* with David McCallum.

Although given second billing, Inger Stevens had a relatively minor role, which was included, as more than one reviewer suggested, to add some irrelevant female interest to the plot. A hard working girl, she had tackled six major films within the space of that year—*The Long Ride Home, The Borgia Stick, A Guide for the Married Man, Firecreek, Madigan,* and *Hang 'Em High.* She became well known to television viewers for her series "The Farmer's Daughter."

*Hang 'Em High,* released in 1968, was another instant success, though predictably enough, *Variety* (July 19, 1968) struck a sour note with its comments: "A poor American-made imitation of a poor Italian-made imitation of an American-made Western," and the review went on to describe the film as "distasteful, largely pointless, loaded with express explicit violence, even ludicrous."

David Austen, writing for *Films and Filming* (London, November 1968), declared that "*Hang 'Em High* has an air of sincere earnestness which the Italian films carefully invert, and so it is far harder to accept its graphic depiction of violence." Of Eastwood's acting, Austen went on to say that his "laconic style . . . does not really suit the more naturalistic tones of his American co-stars." Commenting at the time on the climate of violence in films, Clint Eastwood had this to say: "Maybe violence in films has a relieving effect upon audiences. Westerns to me are escapist entertainment—and there's always shooting—but I agree there is sometimes too much violence. . . . remember, it's show business. All you want is a full house, whether it's cinema or Las Vegas."

Eastwood's Malpaso Company went into action for his next film, *Coogan's Bluff*—a kind of Eastern Western, as several commentators described it. It was the first of his

films to be directed by Donald Siegel, a man who was to
have as much influence on Eastwood's career from that
point on as Sergio Leone had had on his earlier feature
film appearances.

Playing the title role himself, Clint Eastwood assem-
bled a strong supporting cast (often the hallmark of a
Malpaso film) that included Lee J. Cobb, playing a
tough New York police sergeant, and elicited a strong
performance from Don Stroud in the role of Ringerman,
the wanted man.

The story originated with Herman Miller, who wrote
the screenplay with Dean Riesner and Howard Rodman.
The result is a nicely balanced contrast between Walter
Coogan (Clint Eastwood), the slow but sure moving
Arizona deputy cast adrift in the big city (New York),
and Sheriff McCrea, who sent him there to extradite
Ringerman.

Walt Coogan is an instinctive hunter who rarely fails
to track down his prey—human or animal. This makes
him invaluable in his role as deputy sheriff in the wilds of
Arizona's Piute country. Coogan is also a loner, and this
trait often gets him into trouble with his superior, Sheriff
McCrea.

The story opens with Coogan tracking down and
arresting a criminal. On his way back to town, he stops
off to take a bath at the home of one of his admirers,
Millie. McCrea appears and says he has a special assignment for him—to go to New York to extradite James
Ringerman, an escaped Arizona prisoner who is now in
custody.

Used to acting quickly and on his own, Coogan soon
finds himself hampered by the processes of the law in

New York. Detective Lieutenant McElroy tells Coogan that he will have to wait a few days, as Ringerman has taken a dose of LSD and is undergoing treatment at Bellevue hospital. He cannot be moved until he is released by the doctors.

Biding his time, Coogan meets Julie Roth, a probation officer. Restless over the delays in extraditing Ringerman, Coogan then bluffs his way into Bellevue and persuades the attendants to release the man into his custody. Before leaving with the deputy, Ringerman whispers a message to a young girl who has been visiting him.

The nature of the message becomes apparent at the airport when Coogan is called to the phone, only to find himself blackjacked by Ringerman's associates—who then free the prisoner and get away. Coogan recovers consciousness and is faced with an angry McElroy, who tells him to leave the matter to the New York police— 28,000 strong.

Annoyed, Coogan is more determined than ever to find his man and starts off by locating Ringerman's mother. In so doing, he blows a police stake-out. He finds himself in trouble again with McElroy, who hands him a telegram from Sheriff McCrea informing him that he is off the case.

Julie feels sorry for Coogan and invites him to dinner at her apartment. While she is in the kitchen, Coogan leafs through her file of probationers and finds the address of Ringerman's girl friend. At her apartment, he makes love to the girl, and she promises to lead him to Ringerman. Instead she takes him to a pool hall, where Coogan recognizes Pushie, the man who blackjacked him. A fight ensues, during which Coogan defends himself with a billiard cue and eventually escapes through a window. He returns to his cheap hotel to tend his wounds. Furious with himself, he returns to the girl's apartment, kicks open the door, and frightens her into promising to lead him to Ringerman's hideout.

Ringerman is holed up inside the Cloisters in Fort Tryon Park and is armed with Coogan's stolen gun. He shoots at Coogan and then tries to escape on a motorcycle. Coogan follows him on another machine. They collide after a chase, and Coogan brings the wanted man down in a rugby tackle. At this moment the police arrive, led by McElroy, and Coogan—grinning—announces that he is making a citizen's arrest.

The next day, Coogan flies back to Arizona with his man, having made his mark on New York.

The formula is successful, and Coogan is very much an Eastwood role—a loner, a man able to make and carry out his own decision. The film later led to the creation of the "McCloud" television series.

The pivotal role of the police sergeant who is old enough and wise enough to play it by the book falls to Lee J. Cobb. A veteran actor of many film successes, he has to his credit roles in *On the Waterfront*, *Four Horsemen of the Apocalypse*, *How the West Was Won*, *Our Man Flint* and *Mackenna's Gold*, among many others. Curiously enough, his early ambition was to be a violinist, but a broken wrist put an end to his musical career. After some years of studying aeronautics, he decided to try his hand at acting. His first part was a nonspeaking role in *Peer Gynt* at the Pasadena Community Playhouse in California. At twenty-one, he established himself as a powerful character actor in *Crime and Punishment* (playing an old man) and later with Tallulah Bankhead in *Clash by Night*. His most famous screen role is probably in *Twelve Angry Men*, and television viewers will remember him for his portrayal of Judge Henry Garth in "The Virginian."

Don Siegel came to *Coogan* from *Madigan* and many years in television, as well as from directing small low-budget thrillers that have now been recognized as classics of their kind. By the time of the filming of *Coogan*, Siegel was just starting to gain recognition for such films as *Riot in Cell Block 11*.

*Coogan's Bluff* was again extremely violent, a point not overlooked by the critics. Perhaps one of the best appraisals appeared in London's *Films and Filming* (May 1969): "Coog is more than an anti-hero, he is a slob. . . . this cop has so few traces of humanity it might be thought the only claim for the film is as an example of American neo-realism." Tracing the development of Coogan from this insensitive level to a level at which he can feel pity, the reviewer concludes that "it will make a fortune if shown in American supermarkets because it panders heart and soul to the spiritual and material dough of popular American opinion."

*Time* magazine (November 15, 1968), so often an indicator of popular American opinion, did describe the film as "fast, tough and so well made that it seems to have evolved naturally . . . some of the best American moviemaking of the year." The reviewer went on to make what was surely meant as a compliment to Eastwood, stating that Clint "performs with a measure of

real feeling in the first role that fits him as comfortably as
his tooled leather boots."

Following *Coogan's Bluff*, Clint Eastwood flew to
Europe to star with Richard Burton and Mary Ure in
MGM's lavish production *Where Eagles Dare*, shot at
London's Borehamwood Studios and in the Austrian
Alps. The impressive cast included Michael Hordern,
Patrick Wymark (who became the businessman's folk
hero in *The Planemakers* and other television shows),
Robert Beatty, Anton Diffring, and Donald Houston.

The film, shot in Panavision and Metrocolor, cost
MGM a lot of money—Burton is reported to have been
paid $1,250,000, while Clint Eastwood collected a con-
trastingly modest $800,000. (Clint Eastwood's later com-
ments about tight budgets and economic shooting schedules make interesting reading in the light of these
figures).

One of the interesting things about *Where Eagles Dare*
was its direction by a then virtually unknown young
man, Brian Geoffrey Hutton—at the time in his mid-
thirties. He was a former actor, born in Harlem, who
had worked his way through acting school by taking a
variety of odd jobs that included warehouse packer,
laboratory assistant, and agency messenger. In New York
he studied under a number of well-known drama coaches
and appeared in several off-Broadway plays, notably
*Have You Heard This One?*

He then spent a year in London before deciding to
have a go at film directing. Under Universal Studios'
short-lived "new film horizons" film program (designed to

promote new creative talent), he directed *Wild Seed* with producer Albert S. Ruddy. Producer Ross Hunter was impressed by his work and signed him up to direct *The Pad—And How To Use It*, which starred a number of completely unknown actors and actresses.

When he came to direct *Eagles*, producer Hal Wallis had taken Hutton under his wing. He had already appeared as an actor in *Gunfight at the OK Corral*, *Fear Strikes Out*, and *King Creole*. He has also directed *Sol Madrid*. Hutton, of course, went on to direct a subsequent Clint Eastwood film for MGM, *Kelly's Heroes*, but is probably best known for *X, Y, and Zee*.

As for Richard Burton, when one thinks of his roles in *Look Back in Anger, Beckett, Who's Afraid of Virginia Woolf?, The Spy Who Came in from the Cold, Taming of the Shrew*, or *Staircase*, it is hard to understand what persuaded him, apart from the money, to star in *Where Eagles Dare*, playing the part of the stiff-upper-lip British officer who has everything under control. The part did little if anything to add to his stature, and several studio biographies simply do not mention this little digression.

Writer Alistair MacLean had set such a high standard for himself in Carl Foreman's *The Guns of Navarrone* that *Eagles* came as something of a disappointment.

The story centers around an international group of adventurers, each one adept at survival behind enemy lines, who have been parachuted into Germany with an incredible objective: the rescue of a high-ranking Allied officer from a seemingly impregnable castle, which is the secret mountain-top headquarters of the Gestapo in southern Germany. Leading the group of seven men and a woman is John Smith, a quiet man with a genius for extracting information and staying alive under almost any conditions. With him are Montana-born Lieutenant Schaffer of the American Rangers, Olaf Christiansen, Torrance-Smythe, Caraciola, Lee Thomas, and Sergeant Harrard. The lone woman, whose presence is unknown to everyone except Smith (she parachutes into the same area moments after them), is Mary Ellison. She has worked with Smith before on similar missions.

After landing in a nighttime snowstorm, the men gather, only to find that Harrard is missing. After a search, his body is found. He died as the result of a broken neck, and while the rest are convinced that this is the result of a fall, Smith suspects a killer among his own men.

Smith has a secret meeting with Mary Ellison and then leads his men toward the castle—the only means of access is by heavily guarded cable car. Through binoculars, they observe the arrival by helicopter of a high-ranking German officer, which leads them to suspect that every effort will be made now to extract vital information from the prisoner. Time is pressing.

Smith and his party don German uniforms and, in the nearby village, mingle freely with recruits from the crack German alpine corps. Smith makes contact with Heide in a local bar: she is an Allied agent. Mary Ellison arrives, posing as Heide's cousin, ostensibly to start work as a maid inside the castle.

The stage is set to make their strike at the castle when disaster overtakes them. First the body of Torrance-Smythe is discovered. Then a raid on the tavern forces the surrender of Smith and his men. Smith and Schaffer manage to escape by setting fire to the railway station and creating a diversion.

They make their way to the cable car and make a dangerous ascent. Mary is meanwhile inside the castle and having her own problems fending off an ardent German admirer.

The two men carry out their mission and finally escape to safety—this time trying to outwit an enemy surrounding them on all sides.

The critics saw the film as another in the tired-out genre of World War II action films. Richard Schickel, writing for *Life* magazine (March 28, 1969), complained of MacLean that "he is so intrigued by seeing how many twists the basic plot can stand before it—and our attention—breaks under the strain, he neglects some basic obligations. Perhaps most serious is the lack of characterization."

Neither Richard Burton nor Clint Eastwood received glowing notices from the reviewers. Typical of the comments in the press were those of the *Los Angeles Times* (March 13, 1969): "Richard Burton . . . performs with a competent and deadpan sincerity. It cannot have been easy. Eastwood is a drawling yank, slow to comprehend British deviousness. . . . Everyone says the lines and gets on with the physicalities."

Maybe the usefulness of *Where Eagles Dare* from Clint Eastwood's point of view is that it afforded him a sort of trial run for a subsequent war epic, *Kelly's Heroes*, in which it fell to him to lead another band of soldier/desperadoes to a crock of hidden gold.

The film also brought Eastwood into contact with Elizabeth Taylor, and she and Richard Burton and

Eastwood have remained friends ever since. It was Miss Taylor who, spending a lot of time on the set reading through scripts submitted to her, passed Eastwood a screenplay called *Two Mules for Sister Sara*; but more of that later.

In spite of its excellent casting and expensive budget, *Where Eagles Dare* was not a great film and is not a particular landmark in the career of Clint Eastwood.

# 5

## *Paint Your Wagon* and *Kelly's Heroes*

$A$s well as having the ability to climb onto bandwagons, Hollywood is also noted for its incapacity, once on, to know when it is time to get off.

I preface this chapter with these remarks because I think that by 1969 anyone, and I mean anyone, could have predicted that the day of the big screen musical was over. Yet, in spite of this, Paramount poured huge sums of money into what was to be Clint Eastwood's next picture, *Paint Your Wagon*—this film along with another musical, *Darling Lily*, nearly bankrupted them.

On the face of it, *Paint Your Wagon* looked like a good deal. It was produced by Alan Jay Lerner and directed by Joshua Logan. Music was by Lerner and Loewe (embellished—or not, according to taste—by additional material from André Previn). An established stage success, it had a good cast lineup that included Eastwood, Lee Marvin, Jean Seberg, and Harve Presnell.

The story opens on the rugged trail west in the days of the gold rush when hard-drinking, hard-fighting, happy-go-lucky Ben Rumson (Lee Marvin) meets up with quiet-living, introspective Pardner, played by Clint Eastwood. According to Ben: "When I fall dead drunk in the street, I expect you to come and get me; when I owe a man a hundred dollars I expect you to stand good for me; if I am sick, you will nurse me; if I turn melancholy—which can happen out here—then you will be my companion and solace me."

The pair, tireless in their prospecting for gold, grow tired of their womanless world. When Jacob Woodling (John Mitchum), a Mormon Preacher, arrives on the scene with two wives, Elizabeth (Jean Seberg) and Sarah, Ben negotiates the purchase of Elizabeth for his wife—for the sum of $800. Ben is jealous and cannot stand other men ogling his "wife" and almost kills Tabor (William O'Connell) who, he believes, is paying her too much attention.

A meeting is then held, and it is decided to send Ben on a mission to hijack a wagon loaded with six French "ladies" who are on their way to Sonora. The Grisly Bear saloon is refurbished to house the girls—the saloon is to be under the management of Rotten Luck Willie (Harve Presnell). Complications arise when, during Ben's absence, Pardner and Elizabeth fall in love.

Ben is furious and is about to dissolve his partnership with Pardner when Elizabeth confesses that she truly loves both of them. If Woodling could have two wives, there is no reason why she cannot have two husbands.

The trio then settle down to a contented but eventful life, which includes a bullfight and a major gold strike.

With all this going for it, what went wrong? Filmed in the colorful scenery of Oregon, and with its main song entrusted to the lusty voice of a professional (Harve Presnell), the picture went way over budget and simply never recovered its costs at the box office.

Although he had only hit the big time at the age of forty, Lee Marvin was no stranger to moviegoers; for thirteen years or more, he had been one of Hollywood's most dependable actors. Then suddenly his performances in *Ship of Fools*, *Cat Ballou*, the English-made *Dirty Dozen*, and *The Professionals* really awakened audiences to his range and talents. But as Ben in *Paint Your Wagon*, Marvin never really came to life and would be unmemorable except for his lugubrious rendering of the song "Wanderin' Star."

*Paint Your Wagon* did little too for Miss Jean Seberg, a slight blonde lady from Marshalltown, Iowa, who did however redeem herself some months later with her role in *Airport* (as the passenger relations girl).

Her career had been a distinguished one. Although born in the United States, she had lived largely in Paris, her liking for the city aroused during the filming of *Bonjour Tristesse* for Otto Preminger. She married a Frenchman, but the marriage failed after eighteen months. Miss Seberg then went to England to appear opposite Peter Sellers in *The Mouse That Roared*, produced by Walter Shenson. But it was on her return to France, when she started to work consistently with Truffaut and Jean-Luc Godard, that she rose to prominence. There she starred in a low-budget ($70,000) film opposite an unknown young man named Jean-Paul Belmondo—the result was *Breathless* and instant stardom for the Frenchman.

Although Jean Seberg appeared in a number of American-made films—*Lilith* (with Warren Beatty and Peter Fonda), *Moment to Moment*, and *Birds in Peru* (directed by her then husband Romain Gary)—she was happier to be associated with the French "new wave" of young experimental directors. Thus, her decision to star in *Wagon* was a curious one.

Not only was the public response a negative one, but the critics disliked the film as well. As *Newsweek* (October 27, 1969) pointed out, "it was not one movie, but a hundred mini-movies, none of them sustained long enough to hold our interest."

The same reviewer (Joseph Morgenstern) was equally unimpressed by Clint Eastwood, commenting that while Clint rarely spoke in the Leone Westerns, he was now taking "apart his reputation by speaking often and badly, as if the script girl had neglected to give him each succeeding line."

A discussion of *Kelly's Heroes* seems appropriate at this time, even though the film did not chronologically follow *Wagon*. The reason for this is that, following *Kelly*, Clint Eastwood finally appears to have become a little more choosy about the roles he plays. *Kelly* represents the last of the adventure non-roles that he had up until then accepted.

*Kelly's Heroes* was the second Brian Hutton-directed epic in which Eastwood chose to appear. In fact, the screenplay, written by Troy Kennedy Martin (who wrote some of the early "Z-Cars" scripts for British television), has several similarities to the storyline of *Where Eagles Dare.*

It, too, is a World War II tale, taking place some time soon after the Normandy Invasion. As the film opens, Private Kelly, played by Clint Eastwood, captures a German major. Kelly returns with his prisoner to company headquarters, located in a barn that is in a state of chaos, having been accidentally bombarded by its own mortar section. Sergeant Big Joe (Telly Savalas) interrogates the German officer—to find out which are the best hotels in the newly conquered town of Nancy, whether the three-star restaurant is still operating, and where the girls can be found. He is hoping for once to give his battle-weary men a few hours of rest and recreation.

Meanwhile Kelly, his suspicions aroused by the weight of the German's briefcase, takes over the questioning, armed with a bottle of whiskey. Kelly uncovers the fact that the major is in charge of a shipment of gold that he is to take back to Germany. The major is carrying some "samples" with him, but the rest of the bullion is hidden in the town of Clermont, which is still inside German territory.

More shells rain down on the barn headquarters, but Kelly manages to get out with a few gold bars—the German officer does not make it. Captain Maitland (Hal Buckley), the company commander, decides to spend a few days in Paris and gives his men a three-day pass to be spent in the field. Kelly tries to convince the platoon that they should put their passes to good use and go after the gold. He contacts Crapgame (Don Rickles), an exceptionally enterprising supply sergeant, who comes up with food, ammunition, and vehicles for the mission—and who plans to join the group in order to protect his investment.

Oddball (Donald Sutherland) overhears their plans and is allowed to join the group, if he provides three renegade Sherman tanks. Big Joe is reluctantly persuaded to go along, too, to keep an eye on his men and organize the expedition with military precision.

General Colt (Caroll O'Connor) is meanwhile week-ending in a French chateau, unaware of the plans for a mission that will soon disrupt his comfort with cryptic codes and astounding battle reports. In return for a share in the $16,000,000 target, Mulligan agrees to lay on a covering barrage, and under a hail storm of their own shells Kelly and his men crash through the German lines.

The general atmosphere of *Kelly* is not as grim as in *Eagles*, and the strong supporting cast included a number of deadpan comics—Telly Savalas, Don Rickles, and Donald Sutherland (the latter, of course, the hero of *M\*A\*S\*H*). Sutherland's role created the now popular hippie soldier who is in the war for what he can get out of it (the characterization is not a new one—compare Oliver Reed in *Hannibal Brooks*).

Sutherland gained most of his early dramatic experience in England, though he was born in New Brunswick, Canada, where he started work at fifteen as a disc jockey on a local radio station. He majored in English at the University of Toronto and later enrolled in the London Academy of Dramatic Art. His early stage experience included repertory at Perth, and he first appeared on the

West End stage in *August for the People* with Rex Harrison and Rachel Roberts. Other London stage appearances included *The Shewing Up of Blanco Posnet* at the Mermaid Theatre and *The Spoon River Anthology* at the Royal Court.

Sutherland had gotten into films via horror movies (*Castle of the Living Dead, Dr. Terror's House of Horrors*), and then a relatively minor role in *The Dirty Dozen* prepared the way for a number of beatnik/hero roles in *Start the Revolution Without Me* and ultimately *M\*A\*S\*H* alongside Elliott Gould.

Unfortunately by the time of *Kelly's Heroes*, Sutherland had almost outgrown his stock role of the offbeat character trying to screw up the system, and the supposedly "in" dialogue assigned to him tended to come across as a camp, outdated parody of the real thing. (It is interesting to note that one of the minor faults in Clint Eastwood's latest film as director, *Breezy*, is that the hippie characters portrayed are extremely plastic and totally unlike anyone found on Sunset Boulevard.) Undaunted, however, Sutherland rose to higher things in Alan J. Pakula's *Klute*, costarring Jane Fonda.

By contrast, Telly Savalas as the sergeant in *Kelly's Heroes* was a joy to watch. His background, too, is colorful. He was born Aristotle Savalas in Garden City, Long Island, of Greek parents. He completed his education at Columbia University, majoring in psychology, after seeing World War II service. Savalas apparently had no thoughts about becoming an actor and went to work for a branch of the United States Information Agency. He got into broadcasting via the UN/NBC film series, and then David Susskind, mistakenly thinking that Savalas was a seasoned television performer, asked him to appear in a television pilot.

It was Burt Lancaster who spotted him in this and who invited him to play a convict in the now classic *Birdman of Alcatraz*. Savalas then went on to star in *The Young Savages*, *The Battle of the Bulge*, and *The Greatest Story Ever Told* (as Pontius Pilate), to name only a few of his major screen credits. After *Kelly's Heroes* Telly Savalas further distinguished himself in *A Town Called Bastard* and *Pretty Maids All in a Row*.

Clint Eastwood's role in the film called, typically, for a lot of action and not much dialogue. The film was not loved by the critics: Leo Guild in the *Los Angeles Times* (August 17, 1970) called it "the noisiest picture I have ever sat through," and Peter Buckley, writing in London's *Films and Filming* referred to *Kelly's Heroes* as "The Sons of Patton's Dirty Dozen Go Where Eagles Dare." Why, Buckley complained, "was it really necessary to blow half of Yugoslavia for this film?" Buckley further commented that "the acting, with the exception of some predictable mouthing by Eastwood . . . is on an extremely high if broad comedy level."

Maybe Clint Eastwood and his advisers read between the lines, as *Kelly* represents the end of a succession of fairly high-budget, all-action films, and from now on we see Eastwood eschewing Hollywood antics such as these in favor of tighter budgets, smaller casts, and more credible casting. He was now reaching the point at which he could dictate what roles he would play and how he wanted to play them.

As Clint Eastwood himself commented at the time:

"You have to wade through a lot of stuff in order to get a few plums."

# 6

# The Tale of the Nun
# and the Schoolmistress

For his next two films (though we are not
discussing them in strict chronological sequence), Clint
Eastwood submitted again to the direction of Don Siegel.

The first of the two was *Two Mules for Sister Sara* (the
reader will recall that the script was unearthed by
Elizabeth Taylor while her husband and Eastwood were
filming *Where Eagles Dare*). Clint Eastwood had given
the script to Universal Studios, who decided to buy it.

At the same time, Miss Taylor had announced that if
she ever made a Western it would be with Clint
Eastwood. And, indeed, she was originally intended for
the role of the nun who is rescued by Eastwood and who
turns out to be a hooker with a heart of gold.

Producer Martin Rackin had his reservations. "It became too much of a hassle with Liz," he said at the time.

"You have to move half her household to the location and make sure it is near where Burton is working at the time. So I got Shirley MacLaine, who will pack one bag and go anyplace you tell her."

It was unquestionably a dramatic change of role for Shirley MacLaine who came to the film fresh from her success as the taxi dance hostess in *Sweet Charity*. She had never tackled an outdoor adventure role before. In less than four years, she had risen from being an unknown in a Broadway chorus line—understudying Carol Haney in *Pajama Game*—to her first Academy Award-nominated role in MGM's *Some Came Running*, later appearing in *The Apartment*, *My Geisha*, *Two for the Seesaw*, and *What a Way to Go*, among others.

Some observers feel that she was not right for the part in *Two Mules*. She did not seem to be happy at all times on the film set, catching a bad case of influenza and holding up production, declaring that all she wanted to do was to get the film finished and to get the hell back to civilization.

Shirley MacLaine, whose brother is actor Warren Beatty, was born in Richmond, Virginia. Her father had been a musician and bandleader, while her mother taught dramatics at Maryland College. In 1950, before completing high school, Shirley went to New York and got work in the chorus line of *Oklahoma* and *Kiss Me Kate*. She then went back home to finish her schooling but returned to New York again, getting whatever work she could as a demonstrator, dancer, or photographic model. Her success in *Pajama Game* led her to Hollywood and film roles in *Around the World in Eighty Days*, *Can-Can*, *Irma La Douce*, *Two for the Seesaw*, and *Sweet Charity*.

The story of *Two Mules* was set in Mexico at the time of the blood-spattered era of Emperor Maximillian and Benito Juarez. Eastwood plays the part of an American mercenary riding to join the Juaristas to help them take the French garrison at Chihuahua. On his way, he prevents a nude woman from being raped by three drunken bandits, somewhere in the Mexican desert. She turns out to be a nun, Sister Sara, and the two continue their travels together. During a number of adventures, Sara reveals a penchant for cigars, swear words, and liquor, despite her nun's attire.

Between them, they plan to blow up a train carrying supplies to the French. When Eastwood is wounded by an Indian arrow, Sister Sara saves his life and then, as he is too weak, climbs a railway bridge to plant sticks of dynamite in order to blow up the supply train.

Arriving at Chihuahua, they find refuge in a brothel— and Sister Sara's identity as a former hooker is revealed. They join with the Juaristas in destroying the garrison before riding off together.

The film was shot on location in Zapata County, Mexico, and utilized one of the largest sets constructed in that country. With the cooperation of the National Monuments Department of the Mexican government, an entire village was reconstructed, occupying the area of a city block and requiring six months for completion. In the story, a fort that houses a group of Maximillian's soldiers is attacked and destroyed by the Juaristas. The elaborate set was burned down for the ensuing battle scenes.

Some sequences were shot at the nearby Pantitlan and Cauixtla ruins, landmarks of the Mexican revolution. For another sequence, the unit had to reach a bat-infested cave located high on a steep cliff, climbing up on foot, while cameras and heavy equipment were swung up on a specially built cable car.

The arrival of the film company provided something of a field day for the villagers, who earned about four times their normal weekly wages appearing as extras in some of the battle sequences.

When it was discovered that someone had forgotten to include a stunt artist in the crew, Shirley MacLaine earned the applause of the unit as she gamely elected to climb a rail trestle, still dressed in her heavy nun's habit, in the sequence in which she plants explosives to dynamite a troop train.

Eastwood's role as Sara's rescuer is a neat one, and he displayed a nice line in deadpan humor (for example, when they have to share the same horse) that I think comes off. I saw the film at a press showing in London, and the critics seemed to enjoy it; but in Hollywood the trade papers, pursuing what seemed like a personal vendetta against Eastwood, were extremely harsh.

*Variety* (April 13, 1970) declared that "the secret of the spaghetti Western as directed by Sergio Leone was that Eastwood was given more bullets than words in the script. . . . [In *Mules*] Eastwood simply can't act—not in this film anyway."

Even *Time* magazine (July 30, 1970) could not find words of praise for Eastwood's efforts, declaring that "Eastwood looks grizzled, stares into the sun and sneers, but anything more demanding seems beyond his grasp."

It is unfortunate that Clint Eastwood virtually played into the hands of his detractors with his next film, *The*

*Beguiled*. The story takes place somewhere in the South during the last days of the Civil War. A young girl is out picking mushrooms and is shocked to find a wounded Union soldier, Corporal John ("McB") McBurney, played by Clint Eastwood. The soldier's leg is broken just below the knee, but with the help of ten-year-old Amy (Pamelyn Ferdin), the pair manage to make their way to the Farnsworth Seminary for Young Ladies.

The headmistress (Geraldine Page) and her assistant are wondering what to do with the wounded man when a bunch of students rush up to share the excitement. Martha Farnsworth's first reaction is to put the blue flag on the front gate—a signal to passing Confederate soldiers that a Yankee prisoner has been captured. She is dissuaded by Edwina (Elizabeth Hartman) and some of the other girls, who tell her that the graycoats would only imprison the young soldier and leave him to die—the least they can do is tend his wounds before turning him in. The wounded soldier is then carried inside.

McBurney makes a rapid recovery and quickly manages to entice a not-unwilling Carol (Jo Ann Harris) to his bed. When Edwina finds out, she turns on the soldier in a fit of rage and jealousy. Before long she, too, shares the soldier's bed and is thoroughly convinced that he is in love with her. Martha is the next to succumb to McBurney's charm, and even little Amy offers him her pet turtle.

The story takes a tragic turn when the wounded soldier is discovered by Edwina in the act of making love to Carol. The jealous schoolteacher pushes McBurney down the stairs. His injured leg is damaged in the fall, and Martha decides that it must be amputated. After con-

sulting an old medical book, she pours whiskey down the
soldier's throat; and with the help of Edwina and Hallie
(Mae Mercer), she cuts the leg off.

The "operation" is successful; but once recovered,
McBurney is bitter and accuses the women of needlessly
amputating his leg for the sake of keeping him a prisoner
in the seminary. He announces that from now on he is
going to sleep in whatever bed he pleases and drink as
much as he wants and enjoy life at the school. Amy joins
the others in pleading with him to be reasonable, but
McBurney replies by smashing her pet turtle against a
wall.

The headmistress then calls the teachers and pupils
together to try to formulate a plan to get rid of their now
unwanted visitor. Amy is persuaded to go out and gather
poisonous toadstools so that these can be served to the
soldier in place of mushrooms. Meanwhile, McBurney has
undergone a change of heart; during dinner he announces that he plans to marry Edwina. Martha screams
as McBurney collapses and dies.

The next day it appears that Amy did not pick
poisonous mushrooms after all and that McBurney must
have died of a heart attack. The schoolgirls together
make up a patchwork shroud for the dead soldier, their
feelings confused as they realize that he has left their lives
forever.

The film was again directed by Don Siegel and had a
strong all-female cast headed by Geraldine Page in the
role of Miss Martha Farnsworth, headmistress of the
school, who masterminds the plan to get rid of their
unwanted guest. Famous for her interpretations of Tennessee Williams's characters, Geraldine Page makes only

occasional film appearances. Among her most notable are *Taxi* (1953) and *Hondo* (with John Wayne) for which she earned an Academy Award nomination. She received two more for *Summer and Smoke* and *Sweet Bird of Youth* (with Paul Newman). Costarring with her was Elizabeth Hartman (*A Patch of Blue*, *The Group*, *You're a Big Boy Now*, *The Fixer*).

Commenting at the time on his role, Eastwood remarked: "It was quite different from the Westerns I'd been making. There were no bad guys to knock off with blazing guns, no showdowns in the middle of a dirt street, no trusted horse to gallop me to safety when the odds are stacked."

Of *The Beguiled* De Witt Bodeen wrote: "It is not only a different picture for Eastwood but in my opinion it is his best film, in which he gives a real performance, one that has nothing to do with the Man with No Name characterisation or any of the strong but silent Gary Cooper derivatives."

The reviewer in *Time* magazine called the film the most scarifying "since Rosemary birthed her satanic baby." And even *Hollywood Reporter* (March 8, 1971), no admirer of Eastwood's work, declared that "the performances are uniformly excellent, with Clint Eastwood being the most impressive, particularly in the second half of the film in which he is called upon to break with the more passive dimensions of the role and demonstrates a greater versatility and range than his best past work has indicated."

*Motion Picture Exhibitor* (May 5, 1971) also reserved certain words of praise for Eastwood's performance, stating that he "attacks his role with the same plodding shrewdness as an aging Sugar Ray Robinson. In its block-like totality, his is an astonishing though certainly not a great performance."

Judith Crist, in her review for *New York* magazine (April 12, 1971), certainly must have relished writing such lines as "this film . . . is tailored exclusively for sadists and woman-haters. . . . its thesis is that women will calmly kill any man who denies them sexual satisfaction." And "this excrescence is rated R. The family that likes to vomit together can do it at the movies."

Unfortunately the distributors of *The Beguiled* (Universal) were not quite sure how to publicize and distribute the film. It was first announced that it would open at the Picwood in Los Angeles, an important first-run house, and then was canceled the week it was due to open, in spite of heavy build-up publicity. It opened a few weeks later in a number of theaters as part of a double bill.

As sometimes happens, the publicity angles used were evasive, and it was not clear from the catch line, "Clint Eastwood Has Never Been in a More Frightening Situation," that the film was not another Eastwood action picture. Naturally Western addicts were disappointed.

Universal then did another *volte face*, and suddenly all available prints were withdrawn. The film was issued again after a lapse of another few weeks as a solo feature in an art house on Wilshire Boulevard. But the publicity impact had been lost, and the film never managed to pick up.

*The Beguiled* opened in Europe late in 1971. The Paris reviews were quite good—"*Le plus grand du Grand Guignol d'Amerique*"—while the London *Times* called it "a remarkably beguiling film."

As I wrote these notes, *The Beguiled* (along with several other Eastwood films) was enjoying another run in the London suburbs, and *Time Out* (November 16, 1973) wrote: "Eastwood has intruded into a limbo world of Gothic romance . . . we have a film that looks like it could become a forgotten classic of American film, mesmeric, strong and sad."

Not everyone agrees with these views, and among Clint Eastwood's severest critics was Judith Crist. Maybe after being typecast for so long as a gunslinger who said little (jokes abound in Hollywood about Eastwood, e.g., "Don't bother to send him a script, he can't read"), it has taken time for commentators and the cinema-going public to appreciate what he was trying to do with his role in *The Beguiled*.

It is interesting to note that he has never really returned to a part like this, and following *The Beguiled*, he got involved in *Dirty Harry* (another action picture) and *Play Misty for Me*, playing another contemporary role and doubling as director.

1. As the characteristic mean, tough hero, Clint Eastwood stars in **High Plains Drifter** co-starring Verna Bloom, Mariana Hill. Written by Ernest Tidyman and directed by Eastwood himself.

2. The slit-eyed, cigar-chewing Man with No Name is unquestionably Clint's most famous character (shown here in **For a Few Dollars More**).

3. Clint's newly formed Malpaso Company, following the successful formula of the Spaghetti Westerns, co-produced **Hang 'Em High,** in which Clint played the leading role of Jed Cooper.

4. Sticking with the successful ingredient of his previous films, Clint is once again a violent anti-hero in **Coogan's Bluff.**

7. The motley crew of **Kelly's Heroes** sets off on its quest for German gold.

(*Photo © 1970, Metro-Goldwyn-Mayer Inc.*)

8. Clint rescues a woman in distress while on his way to join up with forces in the Mexican Revolution, and not surprisingly is amazed when Shirley MacLaine professes to be a nun.

*(Photo © Universal Pictures)*

9. In **Two Mules for Sister Sara,** Clint looks embarrassingly the same on and off camera.

10. Joe Kidd (Eastwood) and Rita Sanchez (Stella Garcia) arrive in a small village in their pursuit of a dangerous armed group of rebelling Mexican landowners.

(*Photo © Universal Pictures*)

11. Always interested in behind-the-camera aspects of film production, Clint gets a camera's eye view of a **Joe Kidd** scene being filmed on location in Arizona.

*(Photo © Universal Pictures)*

12. Clint gets a camera's eye view of a scene to be photographed inside an automobile for **Breezy.**

# 7

# *Misty* Meets *Dirty Harry*

$F$OR his first shot at directing, Clint Eastwood chose a neat little story, a relatively small cast, and
a plot that lent itself to some attractive outdoor locations.
The result was *Play Misty for Me*.

"After seventeen years of bouncing my head against
the wall," he told columnist Rex Reed, "hanging around
the sets, maybe influencing certain camera setups with
my opinions, watching actors go through all kinds of hell
without any help, and working with both good directors
and bad, I am at a point where I am ready to make my
own pictures."

The idea for *Play Misty for Me* came to Eastwood by
way of a sixty-page treatment submitted to him by Jo
Heims, a young woman Eastwood had known during his
lean years when she had been working as a secretary
while trying to get writing assignments.

The story centers around Dave Garver (Clint Eastwood), a popular disc jockey in the Monterey/Carmel area of California. He finds himself at loose ends when his girl friend, Tobie Williams (Donna Mills), leaves. After his nightly radio spot, Dave frequents a bar—known as the Sardine Factory—which he often mentions on the air. Among the many telephone requests he receives during his show, one is to play "Misty" for a girl caller. The girl is Evelyn Draper (Jessica Walter). One night, she meets Dave at the bar and suggests they spend the night together—with no strings. Dave agrees.

But things do not work out as simply as that. To Dave's increasing annoyance, Evelyn starts dropping in on him uninvited and generally makes a nuisance of herself. When Tobie returns to town and Dave resumes his courtship, Evelyn follows them. Then in a paranoid fit, she gets into Dave's home and knifes Birdie (Clarice Taylor), the cleaning woman, after cutting some clothing and drapes to shreds. Dave returns to find police—led by Sergeant McCallum (John Larch)—all over the place. Birdie is taken to the hospital, and Evelyn is committed to a sanitarium.

Dave thinks that that is the last he has heard of the affair; but some time later, he gets a call from Evelyn—she has left the sanitarium and is on her way to Hawaii. Would he play "Misty" just once more for old times sake? Dave obliges. Later that night at home, he awakens to the tune of "Misty" being played—and narrowly escapes being stabbed by Evelyn, who subsequently escapes.

Evelyn continues to haunt Dave during the next twenty-four hours. When he receives a call from Tobie that she has a new roommate, Dave is suspicious. Lacing a tape recording onto the studio machine, he drives to Tobie's apartment and is just in time to save her from Evelyn.

"*Misty* is an admittedly effective thriller," wrote *Time Out* (November 16, 1973). "It's an uneven film, laced with sexual paranoia, and lingering misogyny. But the tension set up by Eastwood's part makes it puzzling and revealing on a level beyond that of its suspense mechanisms."

The key supporting role of Evelyn Draper is played by Jessica Walter. She is best known for her three-year stint as Julie Morano in the daytime television series "Love of Life."

A native of New York, she trained at that city's High School of Performing Arts and worked her apprenticeship in summer stock and touring productions. She made her Broadway debut in *Advise and Consent* (playing the part of Liz) and then went on to win the Clarence Derwent Award for her performance in Peter Ustinov's *Photo Finish*. She appeared in *Nightlife* and then, as the only American girl in the cast, joined the British production on Broadway of David Merrick's *A Severed Head*.

Her major television roles have been in the Herbert Brodkin series "For the People" and in "Love of Life," but she has made numerous guest appearances in such shows as "The Fugitive," "Mannix," and "The FBI."

The whole of *Play Misty for Me* was shot in and around Carmel on the Monterey Peninsula, an area that Eastwood knows well, as he is building his permanent home there. The scenery is spectacular throughout, and there were sequences shot "as it happened" at the Monterey Jazz Festival.

The film is also memorable for its introduction of

Donald Siegel playing his first role as an actor—as Murphy, the friendly owner of the Sardine Factory.

Perhaps because they felt chastened by their mishandling of *The Beguiled*, Universal gave *Misty* a big build-up, and the film enjoyed a long and successful run at the Cinerama Dome in Los Angeles.

Reviews for *Play Misty for Me* were generally good. David Austen, in *Films and Filming* (London, April, 1972), had to admit that Eastwood's direction was "actually a pretty decent first effort in what can be a tricky genre." And although *Variety* (September 15, 1971) was unhappy about the film's "frequent digressions into landscape," it, too, had to admit that *Misty* is "an often fascinating suspenser" with "generally excellent casting, handsome production, and stretches of good direction by Eastwood."

Eastwood himself told Rex Reed at the time: "At least I know that if it's a failure it's my own fault and not somebody else's. I've been in enough bombs that were somebody else's fault."

With *Dirty Harry*, Clint Eastwood once more reverted to acting only, and Don Siegel took over once again as director. *Dirty Harry* is a fast-moving police thriller, contemporary in content, and shot entirely on location in San Francisco, Eastwood's home town. Clint played the lead role, Detective Harry Callahan, the man they all turn to when there is a particularly nasty job to be done.

As the film opens, we are on a San Francisco rooftop as a sniper takes aim and shoots an arbitrary victim, a girl swimming in a rooftop pool on a nearby building. The killer, who signs himself Scorpio, then demands a ransom

of $100,000 from the city and threatens that if he is not
paid other victims will die—including a Catholic priest
and a black.

In the mayor's office, Detective Harry Callahan is
advised by Lieutenant Bressler (Harry Guardino) that
they are going to pay off the killer. But even before he
can start on the case, Harry is wounded in the leg during
a shootout with some would-be bank robbers. Against his
wishes, he is assigned a partner, Chico (Reni Santoni), an
eager young cop who cannot understand Harry's surly,
negative attitude. Later that night when Harry and
Chico go on patrol, Harry is called for another "dirty
job"—this time talking down a man threatening to throw
himself off a building.

The hunt for the sniper continues. He is spotted by a
police helicopter but escapes and later claims another
victim, a young black boy. Harry is convinced that the
killer will return to the area to carry out his threat to kill a
priest. The sniper is again spotted but escapes following a
gun battle.

Then another note arrives from Scorpio—he has kid-
naped a young girl and buried her alive with just
sufficient air for a short period. If the girl is to live, the
city must pay a ransom of $200,000. Reluctantly Harry
agrees to act as a messenger, and equipped with a small
walkie-talkie, he keeps in touch with his partner Chico.
The sniper orders Harry all over the city, and eventually
they end up in Mount Davidson Park.

The sniper appears, wearing a stocking mask, and tries
to snatch the money from Harry who manages to stab
him in the leg. The man escapes and later inquiries reveal
that he was treated in a hospital near the park. The

doctor thinks the man lives in the keeper's quarters at Kezar Stadium. Harry races to the stadium and locates the sniper, whom he insists on questioning on the spot in an attempt to save the girl's life. But the police are too late to save the girl, and the district attorney is forced to release the sniper on the grounds that the police have infringed upon his constitutional rights.

Determined to bring him to justice, Harry starts to tail the youth, who retaliates by complaining of police harassment. Then, as Harry feared, the youth steals a gun and holds up a school bus loaded with children. He forces the driver at gunpoint to start toward the airport and sends a message to the mayor demanding that a plane and cash be made ready for him.

This time Harry refuses to take the ransom money and, instead, starts off on his own. He manages to jump onto the roof of the bus from a rail bridge and chases the killer through an abandoned factory. He finally corners him and shoots him dead.

When the police arrive, Harry takes off his badge and tosses it into a nearby quarry pond.

Warner Brothers had first acquired the script of *Dirty Harry* with Frank Sinatra in mind for the lead role. But Sinatra had suffered an injury to his hand and was unable to contemplate a part that called for a lot of action.

Eastwood had no such difficulty; in fact, he refused the services of a stuntman and insisted on mounting a fireman's turntable ladder in the scene in which he talks down the would-be suicide. It was also Eastwood who leaped onto the moving school bus from an overhead rail bridge.

Clint Eastwood directed the nighttime suicide sequence himself when Don Siegel became ill. The segment was completed in one night, although six nights had been set aside for it. Working on location in a busy American city is not without its problems, but Clint Eastwood kept his cool throughout, signing autographs and generally making himself available to fans and the press. He is reported to have erupted only once when he jokingly fired a blank pistol shot over the head of a young lady who absolutely refused to leave the set fast enough.

*Dirty Harry* was a typical Eastwood role, cool, sharp, self-sufficient, with not a few parallels with Steve McQueen's performance in *Bullitt*. The film also set a new standard for violence in contemporary cinema, a point that was not overlooked by the reviewers who are quoted here. However, *Dirty Harry* grossed some $22,000,000 and spawned a sequel, *Magnum Force* (1973).

Even in its condemnation of the film as "specious phoney glorification of police and criminal brutality," *Variety* (December 22, 1971) felt obliged to add that it was "a serviceable programmer for general action audiences plus extremists, sadists, revolutionaries and law and order freaks."

Other critics were not so certain of the negative values of *Dirty Harry*. For example, Gordon Gow, writing for London's *Films and Filming* (June, 1972), claimed that "it becomes apparent that *Dirty Harry* is a film of great depth not only engaging us with thriller tactics but positively seething underneath with social criticism. The danger is that many people will keep on seeing things from Harry's viewpoint."

# 8

## *Joe Kidd*
## and *High Plains Drifter*

Wɪᴛʜ *Joe Kidd*, Clint Eastwood returned
to the kind of cowboy action role that had helped make
him an international star. Another joint Malpaso/Uni-
versal venture, *Joe Kidd* had a stong cast lineup that
included Robert Duvall, John Saxon, Don Stroud (he
played the wanted Ringerman in *Coogan's Bluff*), Stella
Garcia, and John Wainwright. The director was John
Sturges.

*Joe Kidd* is an original screenplay by Elmore Leonard
and is set in Mexico at the turn of the century. The story
hinges on the issue of landownership on the American
side of the border. In an effort to protect their interests,
the Mexican-Americans—led by Luis Chama (played by
John Saxon)—present their claims to a prejudiced judge
in the town of Sinola.

When it appears that their claim is going to be thrown out, the Mexican-Americans stage a riot, burning valuable records at the land office and threatening the life of the judge. Joe Kidd (Eastwood), sleeping off a drunken bout in jail, manages to get the judge away to safety.

Some time later, Frank Harlan (Robert Duvall), a big time landowner, arrives in town, bringing with him an entourage of gunmen, and determined to end opposition to his land claims once and for all. Joe Kidd joins the group as a tracker. The party grows in strength and sets off in pursuit of Luis Chama, who is now in hiding.

Harlan's use of a trap to lure Chama causes Joe Kidd to change sides, and he joins up with the Mexicans. In an ensuing range war, Joe Kidd and the Mexicans are victorious. Chama is then persuaded to return to Sinola and allow justice to take its course.

Once again Eastwood is cast in the role of the man who intervenes, siding first with the American land-grabbers and then with the dispossessed Mexicans, remaining with each group just long enough to cause havoc. The reader should not be surprised if he perceives certain similarities with earlier Eastwood roles.

*Joe Kidd* was shot in the Sierras, not far from Bishop, California, and in Tucson, Arizona. Much of the film's authentic atmosphere is derived from Elmore Leonard's expert knowledge of frontier drama: he wrote the novel on which *Hombre* (with Paul Newman) was based as well as the screenplay for *Valdez Is Coming* (starring Burt Lancaster).

Director John Sturges's fascination with loner/heroes is well known from films such as *Bad Day at Black Rock*, *Gunfight at the OK Corral*, *Last Train from Gun Hill*, and *The Magnificent Seven*—all of them Western themes with a moral. *Joe Kidd* is not his greatest film—perhaps, as one reviewer suggested, it lies midway between *The Magnificent Seven* and *The Hallelujah Trail*—and yet he brings to it his special brand of scenic grandeur and love of action (for example, the railway engine sequence). Sturges tends to pick his subjects with care, and it is interesting to speculate just how well *Joe Kidd* might have fared at the hands of another director.

The role of the powerful American landowner fell to Robert Duvall, who at the time was riding on the crest of the wave following his success in *The Godfather* and *The Great Northfield, Minnesota, Mining Raid*, in the last named playing the part of Jesse James. He is an actor whose roles are not always memorable instantly—for example, how many cinemagoers recall that he played Sally Kellerman's lover in *M\*A\*S\*H*? *Time* magazine summed up his screen persona when it wrote: "Engrave his face on a newly minted nickel, and he would still not be recognized in the streets."

Robert Duvall was born in 1932 in San Diego, California, and went to college in Illinois before serving two years in the army. He then worked for the U.S. Post Office to help pay his way through drama school in New York. His efforts paid off, and he appeared in Arthur Miller's *A View from the Bridge* before going on to create the role of Harry Rote in *Wait Until Dark* off-Broadway.

But it was an appearance on television in "Naked City" that brought him to the attention of Hollywood. One of his first film roles was the strange Boo Radley in *To Kill a Mockingbird*. Duvall also played memorable roles in *Bullitt* with Steve McQueen and as John Wayne's adversary, Ned Pepper, in *True Grit*. But his real triumph was as Tom Hagen, the lawyer in *The Godfather*.

John Saxon leads the rival group of Mexican-Americans in the part of Louis Chāma. In order to make the film, he had to take time off from his long-running television series "The Bold Ones." A former male model, Saxon's many film credits include *The Appaloosa* and *Death of a Gunfighter*.

For an interesting appraisal of Eastwood's role of the uncommited loner—and its implications—I commend Arthur Knight's comments for *Saturday Review* (July 29, 1972): "In the past, Western heroes were men who made a commitment—to the cattlemen . . . the victims of oppression, whatever. Eastwood's commitment, however, is solely to himself and to justify this both sides are depicted as rotten. . . . the implications remain. [The film's] creators are men who have no sympathies, no commitments; for them, the entire world is corrupt."

Gordon Gow, in his review for London's *Films and Filming* (November, 1972), notes that the film "lets us know that the dividing line between right and wrong cannot always be drawn with a firm clear flourish. Kidd himself, unlike old time Westerners . . . is just a guy with more going for him personally than the average *hombre*, with no more brilliance of brain than the next man."

A hard-working Clint Eastwood then decided to have another shot at directing and acting in his own film (a repeat exercise from *Play Misty for Me*), and for his next subject returned to the Western genre with *High Plains Drifter*. It was his tenth film as star, his second as director.

Ernest Tidyman, Academy Award winner for *The French Connection*, created the principal role in *Drifter* especially with Clint Eastwood in mind. Certainly there are familiar throwbacks to the almost stock plot of the mysterious stranger who rides into town and gradually succeeds in turning the citizens against each other. And once again there is a kind of moral twist to the story.

The action takes place in the 1870s, and donning the flat-crowned tilted black hat, Clint Eastwood rides into the township of Lago—an opening sequence several minutes long during which the only sounds are the creaking of leather and the jingle of spurs, the only action the frightened and curious stares of the townspeople as they observe the Stranger.

When three of the townspeople try to insult him, shots are quickly fired and the three fall dead. Mordecai Fortune (Billy Curtis) watches in amazement and attempts to befriend the Stranger.

At the local hotel, the Stranger takes a room and soon falls into an exhausted sleep. During a dream sequence, we get our first hint of his mission: a man falls to the ground as a curling bullwhip jerks him off his feet. In the darkness, three shrouded figures continue to whip the man, who reaches out to the onlookers pleading for help. But they stand mute and unyielding. The man is whipped to death.

Meanwhile, the owners of the Lago Mining Company are discussing how to defend the town against three men who are due out of jail and who will be descending on the town seeking revenge against the people who testified against them. They approach the Stranger, who agrees to help them. Meanwhile he learns that the present sheriff received his badge when U.S. Marshal Jim Duncan was whipped to death.

Preparations for the arrival of the convicts upset the inbred routine of the town, and the people begin to suspect that the Stranger is making a mockery of them. During the preparations, Mordecai relives an agonizing past experience—the three convicts administering a whipping to the fallen marshal with the townspeople as witnesses to the deed.

The Stranger's final astonishing command to the people of Lago is literally to paint the town red—and he himself alters the sign on the outskirts to read "Hell."

With the whole town on the alert, the Stranger rides out slowly, leaving Mordecai to signal the start of the ambush. But when the three convicts ride into town, the ambush collapses. By nightfall, they have taken over the town, and there are many dead. But as one of the three men steps out into the darkness, a bullwhip wraps itself around his neck. He is whipped to death. So, too, is the second man. As the third convict aims a gun at the Stranger, who is wielding the whip, he is shot by Mordecai.

The Stranger then rides out of town the way he came in, his mission accomplished.

The entire film was shot on a specially constructed set on the shores of Mono Lake in California, some 300 miles from Hollywood. (For those who like statistics, this involved a forty-six man crew of technicians and ten laborers working twelve hours a day for eighteen days. They used 150,000 board feet of lumber for the job.) In the final sequence when the gunmen come to town, the entire set is burned down.

I found the newness of the buildings slightly disconcerting and for once would have approved of the whole film's being shot on the Universal back lot.

Unusual for an Eastwood film, *High Plains Drifter* has no really strong supporting roles, though Verna Bloom (who made her Hollywood debut in *Medium Cool*) was a delight as Sarah Belding; and Billy Curtis was excellent in the role of Mordecai, a four-feet-two-inch sixty-three-year-old midget who befriends the Stranger and is temporarily installed by him as mayor of Lago.

Critical opinion was once again not very enthusiastic. Describing Eastwood's direction as "mechanically stylish," *Variety* (March 26, 1973) went on to make the following statement: "Pulp magazine mysticism, banal sight gags and spray-on psychedelics are forced into what appears to be an attempt to extend the dimensions of a film formula which in reality has nowhere to go."

London's *Time Out* (September 14, 1973) admitted that *High Plains Drifter* "does run into trouble with Ernest Tidyman's script which seems often at odds with the direction. But it is surreal and mysterious and suggests quite a lot about playing the role of misogynist hero."

Margaret Tarratt, writing for London's *Films and Filming* (October, 1973), would take issue with this last statement as she states in her review that the film "is not even surreal despite the apparent scope for such images. ... The whole thing is an exercise in rhetoric which falls rather flat, despite the stylish camera work."

# 9

## *Breezy*—
## and a New Eastwood Era?

Never a person to stick at one thing for
long, Eastwood surprised the Hollywood motion picture
community once again in 1973 when he decided to direct
*Breezy*. The event marked something of a high point in
his directorial career.

Fresh from *Play Misty for Me* and *High Plains Drifter*
—where he doubled as director and star—Eastwood
chose a gentle, contemporary love story for his first effort
in which he stayed strictly behind the camera. His
decision is praiseworthy on a number of counts: although
certainly different, *Misty* was a suspense-filled drama,
and Eastwood fitted into the role of laconic deejay Dave
Garland with characteristic ease; and *High Plains
Drifter*, not loved by all the critics, was pretty close to the
sort of thing he had been doing since his meeting with

Sergio Leone, though this particular tale did carry a moral.

But with *Breezy*, Eastwood could not help assure the film's success by introducing his own acting talents—a courageous decision by someone whose name on the acting credits means money at the box office. Also, he chose a film that is quite unlike anything he has acted in, let alone directed, before. Finally, his casting shows both imagination and courage. It is not easy for a younger man and comparative newcomer to handle an actor of the experience and status of William Holden. And as if to multiply his problems, Eastwood also accepted the challenge of directing the major motion picture debut of newcomer Kay Lenz, who plays the title role of Breezy.

*Breezy* is the second script that Eastwood has taken from Jo Heims. She wrote the story and, along with Dean Riesner, also the screenplay of *Play Misty for Me*. *Breezy* is her original screenplay, and Heims also served as associate producer.

*Breezy* is the story of a love affair between a middle-aged divorcé, Frank Harmon (played by William Holden), and a young hippie girl, Breezy (Kay Lenz). The two bump into each other outside Harmon's house. The girl is wandering around California, and Harmon agrees to give her a lift down the hill to the main road—partly because he wants to get rid of her from in front of his property. Since Breezy has just dodged the advances of another motorist, she is in a nervous state and annoys Harmon with her nonstop conversation.

As they are nearing the bottom of the hill, Breezy jumps out of the car to go to the aid of a dog that apparently has been injured in a car accident. Harmon says that there is nothing he can do and drives off, but he returns a moment later to pick up the injured animal.

We now meet some of Frank's acquaintances and learn something about him. He runs a real estate office, and despite the attempts by some of his customers—among them Betty Tobin (Marj Dusay), to whom he is showing a house—to make advances, he persists in his determination to stay uninvolved, detached from people.

Later at home, Harmon is juggling his household accounts when the doorbell rings and Breezy appears— she has left her guitar behind in his car. She talks her way into the house and persuades Frank to let her take a bath. When he refuses to let her stay the night, she stalks off out into the rain. Frank tries none too successfully to put the girl out of his mind. The following night he has some more callers—two policemen who have picked up Breezy, whom they have found wandering in the hills. She has told them that she is Frank's niece, and he decides to go along with the story.

Breezy then persuades Frank to drive down to the beach—she has been in California for three months and has never seen the ocean.

In spite of himself, Frank finds himself getting more and more involved with Breezy. On the second night, he finds her waiting in his bedroom and they make love. The next day, Frank has a surprise for Breezy when they drive to a nearby animal hospital to pick up the dog that Breezy thought was dead. He is christened Sir Love-A-Lot, and the three become a happy trio.

There are some embarrassing meetings with some of Frank's older, sophisticated friends, and his doubts about the wisdom of their relationship are increased still more as he watches Breezy fooling around with her young friends. He tells Breezy their affair is over.

An automobile accident involving Betty Tobin's husband awakens him to the sense of loss, and he drives from the hospital to Plummer Park to find Breezy and take up where they left off.

Eastwood's liking for location filming is well known. We have discussed the fact that he chose the Monterey Peninsula as the setting for *Misty* and Mono Lake, with its unusual wasteland and moonscape scenery, as the location for *High Plains Drifter*. If Monterey is his backyard, so, too, is Los Angeles where he maintains a town house in Sherman Oaks, a few minutes drive from the Universal lot.

Eastwood and his colleagues spent several weeks scouting for locations—moviegoers who know Los Angeles will recognize Laurel Canyon, Nichols Canyon, Lookout Mountain, Topanga Canyon, Pacific Coast Highway, Marina Del Rey, Kirkwood Avenue, Plummer Park, Griffith Park, Hollywood Boulevard, and Ventura Boulevard, among the many locations used for the film.

## William Holden

It is Holden who plays the part of Frank Harmon, a not unattractive fifty-year-old divorcé who falls in love with Breezy, a seventeen-year-old hippie. Holden is a man of many parts, and his career is an interesting one. As well as acting in films, he is a successful businessman with interests in a wide range of ventures including import-export, electronics, mini radios, television sets, racetrack investments, and hotels and clubs that take him annually many miles around the world. In spite of all this, his early career was modest enough.

He was born in O'Fallon, a small town in Illinois, and his parents' name was Beedle. His father was fairly prosperous—a manufacturing chemist—and when young William was three, the family moved to Pasadena, California. While attending Pasadena Junior College, he acted in student theatricals; this, in turn, led to small parts at the Pasadena Playhouse. It was there that he was spotted by a studio talent scout who urged him to take a screen test for Paramount, where he was eventually placed under long-term contract.

The year was 1938 when Holden won his first lead role as the young boxer in Rouben Mamoulian's film *Golden Boy* for Columbia—an event that reinforced his decision not to return to college and study chemistry.

Like a number of contract actors of his day, Holden— and he was now renamed after a William Holden who was at the time assistant managing editor of the *Los Angeles Times*—was shuffled between a number of studios, notably Columbia and Paramount. In 1941, while filming *Arizona* for Columbia, he married actress Brenda Marshall on July 13.

When the United States entered World War II, Holden was among the first to enlist, joining as a private in the air force. He emerged four year later as a first lieutenant, returning to Hollywood in 1945. It was not easy settling down, and as well as chasing and securing a wide number of roles, Holden took an active part in the affairs of the film colony. He was on the board of directors of the Screen Actors Guild and was a member of the

Veterans Affairs Committee that helped to place returning actors in screen roles, especially helping small and bit part actors.

He also got involved in the Permanent Charities Committee and the Motion Picture Industry Council and served as a delegate for the Screen Actors Guild at AFL conventions in San Francisco and Houston.

Holden's film career was active and varied. In 1950, he received an Academy Award nomination for his role in *Sunset Boulevard*; and three years later, he won the Best Actor Oscar for his rousing performance in *Stalag 17*. His other memorable roles were in *The Moon Is Blue*, *Dear Wife*, *Streets of Laredo*, *Executive Suite*, *The Bridges at Toko-Ri*, *The Country Girl*, *Love is a Many-Splendored Thing*, *Bridge on the River Kwai*, *The Horse Soldiers*, *The World of Suzie Wong*, and *The Wild Bunch*.

Although Holden was not an obvious choice for the role in *Breezy*, his performance should open up a whole new career for him as a major character actor—if he can find time between other engagements and the annual six-month visit he makes to his Mount Kenya Safari Club in East Africa (where he keeps a ranch of over 300 different species of animals).

## Major debut for Kay Lenz

An even less obvious choice was made for the title role of *Breezy*—a young actress, Kay Lenz. Here again Eastwood showed that he is very much his own man, even when it comes to casting. After Eastwood had screen tested numerous young women put forward by every Hollywood agent with a female on its books (a chore that Holden performed daily with patient stoicism), it was Bob Daley who spotted Lenz on a television "Movie of the Week," *The Weekend Nun*. Daley then brought her to the attention of a grateful Eastwood.

Kay was born in 1953 in Los Angeles and is the daughter of Ted Lenz, actor, producer, writer, and commentator on radio and television. Her mother, Kay Miller, was a professional model (the "Miller High Life" girl) and appeared on television with Lawrence Welk.

Kay made her television debut in 1953—at the age of eight weeks! Her father was producing the Al Jarvis "Hollywood on Television" show, and it was decided that guest Dottie O'Brien, a Capitol recording artist, should hold a real baby in her arms while crooning a lullaby. Little Kay accepted the part with apparent gusto, howling all the way through the singer's performance. Her first television appearance, however, brought fan mail. From that time on, she literally grew up before the television cameras, often appearing in commercials directed by her father as well as doing guest performances on children's and teen-agers' shows. When she was eleven, she acted and sang in *My Genie and Me*, a little theater musical that ran for over 150 performances. Two years later, she played eight weeks at the Pasadena Playhouse in *Dark of the Moon* with Henry Darrow and Monte Markham.

When Kay was fourteen, she appeared on "The Monroes" and in the Andy Griffith and Tammy Grimes television shows. She then left television work to complete her education at Milliken Junior High School in Van Nuys and Grant High School, graduating in 1972.

She returned to acting with assignments in Universal's *American Graffiti* and in *Playmates*, an ABC "Movie of the Week." She also had a featured role in an "Ironside" segment—and, of course, the role in *Weekend Nun* that brought her to the notice of Clint Eastwood.

Up to this time, Kay had used the professional name of Kay Ann Kemper, but she decided to return to her family name for *Breezy*.

## Important supporting role for Marj Dusay

One of the hallmarks of an Eastwood film is the strength of the supporting roles. In *Breezy*, Marj Dusay brings her considerable talents to the part of Betty Tobin, the woman who is in love with Holden and whose husband's death in a car crash forces him to realize his love for Breezy. A native of the small town of Hayes, Kansas, Marj Dusay made her way to San Francisco where she acted in theater before taking numerous parts in films and television. Her television credits include "Get Smart," "Daniel Boone," "Felony Squad," "Hawaii Five-O," "Hogan's Heroes," and "Star Trek"; while motion picture roles included *Clambake* (with Elvis Presley) and *Pendulum*.

Now one of the busiest young actresses in Hollywood, Miss Dusay has recently guest-starred in "The FBI," "Cannon," and "Alias Smith and Jones."

## Other leading roles and staff for *Breezy*

As ex-star of television's long-running "Rawhide" series himself, Eastwood is apparently a great believer in television as a proving ground for many of the top young actors and actresses of today. Tight schedules in television production mean that actors have to learn fast and take direction. Thus, in casting, it should be no surprise that Eastwood seems to lean toward television as a resource for many of the minor supporting roles in his films. *Breezy* was certainly no exception, and the cast list includes a string of well- and less well-known television actors.

They include Dennis Olivieri, who plays the role of Bruno, the young hippie who befriends Breezy. Olivieri starred in *The Naked Ape* for Universal and has been featured on television in "The Whole World Is Watching" and "The New People." Jamie Smith Jackson plays Marcy, Breezy's closest girl friend. A former New York actress, she came to the part from the starring role of Alice in *Go Ask Alice*, another ABC "Movie of the Week." Roger C. Carmel, who plays the part of Henderson—a good friend who makes Holden realize the difference in ages between himself and Breezy—is a veteran television actor, best known for "The Mothers-in-Law" series. His wife is played by Shelley Morrison, a featured actress on the now defunct "Flying Nun" series. Eugene Petersen comes from the "Medical Center" television show, as well as episodes for "The FBI" and "Mannix." Joan Hotchkiss has been a regular on "The Odd Couple," costarring with Tony Randall and Jack Klugman.

There is even a part in the film for Holden's son Scott (playing the part of the veterinary surgeon who saves the life of the dog), who has appeared in "The Revengers" with his father. Perhaps the only completely unknown actor was the dog, Sir Love-A-Lot, a German wire-haired pointer—real life name, Earle.

Eastwood also stuck to known associates in picking his crew members. Cameraman Frank Stanley worked on

*Misty* and *The Beguiled*. The first assistant director worked on *Joe Kidd* and *High Plains Drifter*. Ferris Webster edited both these films; sound man James Alexander worked on *Drifter*; and art director Alexander Golitzen worked on *Joe Kidd*.

## The critical response

A sampling of the reviews for *Breezy* indicates that, although not overwhelmingly favorable to the Jo Heims script, the critics were impressed by Eastwood's development as a director. Various reviews labeled the film "an okay contemporary drama," "more like a television feature . . . than a gripping and certainly relevant . . . sudser," "a cleaned-up middle-American version of *Last Tango in Paris*," and "a mediocre movie."

Noting the different kind of movie Eastwood had chosen to direct and the different kind of performance he had to elicit from his cast, *Variety* (October 29, 1973) declared that Eastwood had not sustained the dramatic mood of the film "failing on the side of restraint (to put it gently) or else inarticulated shallowness of character development and emotional expression (to lay it out plainly)." However, the reviewer went on to state that he could see a definite improvement in Eastwood's direction, going so far as to say, "he's on his way. Maybe next time."

Although Alan R. Howard, writing for the *Hollywood Reporter* (October 30, 1973), detected "a certain fuzziness in the director's attitude to the story," he could say that "Eastwood's first two movies . . . proved him to be a careful film-maker often passionately engaged in the medium's power."

Even Kevin Thomas (*Los Angeles Times*, November 11, 1973) found Eastwood's direction to have merit. Noting that although "most actors develop a hankering to direct . . . few have done so as successfully as Clint Eastwood who all the while has held onto his No. 1 spot at the box office." Thomas went on to say that although Eastwood's first two films borrowed from other directors, "he has made a deeply felt, fully realized film that is entirely his own."

# 10

# Malpaso and the People around Eastwood

Iт is not uncommon for a major star to form a production company. Usually the reasons include a need to hedge against high taxation, and the resulting corporation does little more than hire out the services of its owner. This is certainly not the case with Malpaso, the company formed by Clint Eastwood in 1968, and which has some kind of connection with every film he now makes. Additionally, the Malpaso Company gets involved in projects in which Eastwood stars, stars and directs, directs only, or in which he may take nothing more than a financial interest. Malpaso is very much alive.

It also reflects in a number of ways the characteristics of its owner, from the modest offices it occupies to the type of people who work for and with Eastwood.

Basically, the company is run out of Eastwood's bunga-
low dressing-room-cum-office on the Universal Studios
back lot (he is located next to Lucille Ball) and from a
two-room complex across the road in what used to be a
motel (now occupied by Universal to house overflow
personnel). The whole operation is tightly knit and personal and revolves around Eastwood, director Don
Siegel, producer Bob Daley, and Malpaso story editor
Sonia Chernus.

## Don Siegel

A lot is starting to be written about Don Siegel, the
director most often used by Eastwood, particularly in
recent movies, and the man who directed *Coogan's Bluff*,
*Two Mules for Sister Sara*, *The Beguiled*, and *Dirty
Harry*. He also had an intriguing cameo role as a
bartender in Eastwood's first film as director—*Play Misty
for Me*.

Don Siegel was born in Chicago on October 26, 1912,
and is the son of Samuel Siegel, the finest mandolin
virtuoso of the time. Don's education was varied and
international; he attended a series of state schools in New
York City and then moved to England with his parents,
where he studied for a while at Cambridge.

At the age of twenty, he took off for Paris and lived the
bohemian life of the Left Bank for a few months. He had
ideas about becoming a painter, and then, apparently
realizing that he had little talent for it, gave up the
notion and looked for fresh directions for his energy.

His father's fortunes had meanwhile dwindled, and
the young Donald decided to return to America. He
achieved this by working his passage on a number of

ships bound for the Orient, and eventually he found himself in Los Angeles, worn out and completely broke.

Virtually his sole contact in the city was an uncle. The latter took the youngster under his wing and within a short time had introduced him to Hal B. Wallis. Shortly thereafter, Siegel got his first job inside the movie business—as a film librarian. In time he started to move up the ladder, becoming, in turn, film editor and director of inserts and then head of Warner Brothers' montage department.

He was given virtually free range and spent some of the happiest and most productive years of his life in this little known field of film making. He also worked as a second unit director, getting some of his first experience in heavy action sequences and starting to develop a style that he would make all his own in later years.

In 1945, after the war, Siegel directed two shorts for Warners—*Stars in the Night* (a film about the birth of Christ) and *Hitler Lives?* Both films were accorded Academy Award Oscars.

A year later, he launched his career as a full-fledged director with the film *The Verdict*, starring Sydney Greenstreet and Peter Lorre. He followed this with *Night unto Night*.

It was shortly after this that Siegel demonstrated a characteristic streak of independence that probably has contributed in no small way to keeping him out of favor with big-time Hollywood production companies (and, by the same token, endearing him to Eastwood and Malpaso). Howard Hughes, who had acquired the RKO studios, asked him to salvage his production of *Vendetta*, but Siegel refused on the grounds that the film was beyond help. Hughes evidently was impressed by Siegel's forthright attitude and subsequently hired him to direct *The Big Steal*, starring Robert Mitchum.

Siegel was clearly on his way. One of his specialties was to turn fairly low-budget film fare into minor screen classics. *The Invasion of the Body Snatchers*, for instance, overcame its unworthy title and is now widely regarded as one of the most stylish and intelligent of all science fiction films.

Carefully picking his films and turning his hand to only one or maybe two productions annually, Don Siegel directed a string of memorable titles, including *Crime in the Streets*, *Baby Face Nelson*, *Hell Is for Heroes*, and *Madigan*. He has also worked, though considerably less spectacularly, on a number of American television productions.

It was the later Eastwood films—in particular *Dirty Harry*—that helped turn Siegel into something of a cult director, a position that was enhanced with *Charley Varrick*, starring the inimitable Walter Matthau.

Among film buffs in Europe, Siegel ranks alongside directors of the stature of Godard (though he swears he has never seen a Godard movie), Truffaut, Antonioni, de Sica, and Visconti—not bad company to be in at any time. Siegel's work has been noted and commented on for the past decade by the French *Cahiers du Cinema*, and in London the National Film Theatre has held at least one retrospective of his films.

Outside Hollywood, where money probably talks loudest, he has not gone entirely unnoticed in the United States. Leading universities with film departments—Dartmouth, Loyola, USC, and UCLA among them—

invite him to speak at screenings of his early films. The University of Boston's Mungar Memorial Library houses a comprehensive selection of his manuscripts, scripts, papers, notes, and correspondence.

Siegel is typically sanguine about this latter day acclaim—which contrasts poignantly with his status inside the film capital where he has been working for over thirty years. He talks about being "without honor, like a prophet in his own land" and stresses that "the important thing is to keep going."

He is not a particularly easy man to work with and is known as a battler for what he thinks is right or real in movie making. He rarely, if ever, bawls out actors, but many a producer has breathed a sigh of relief when the shooting of a Siegel film comes to a close.

Siegel lives modestly enough in Sherman Oaks, not far from Eastwood's own simple weekday home. He has a son, the young actor Kristoffer Tabori, by his first marriage to Viveca Lindfors. Kristoffer, who is now in his early twenties, gained considerable fame when he opened as one of the stars in the David Merrick Broadway stage production of *The Penny Wars*. Kristoffer's first film role was in Twentieth Century-Fox's *Making It*, which was filmed in 1970. Don Siegel's second wife is the former Doe Avedon, and the couple have four children— Nowell, Ann, Katherine, and Jack.

Nurtured on films with low budgets and unpretentious plots and casting, it is not surprising that Don Siegel found himself in close rapport with Eastwood when they came together in 1968 for *Coogan's Bluff*, though Siegel reportedly considers *The Beguiled* as his favorite work with Eastwood.

Both on and off location, the pair enjoy a comradeship and mutual respect for each other's professional capabilities. Clint may rib his director friend about particular shots that he labels "siegelese," but with typical friendliness, Eastwood included Siegel as an actor when he first tried his hand at directing in *Misty*.

### Robert Daley

The name of Bob Daley now appears almost invariably in the list of credits for any Malpaso Company film. He was the producer of *Breezy*, starring William Holden, and had acted as production executive on five previous films.

Daley joined the Malpaso outfit in January, 1970, to serve as an executive or producer on all motion picture productions, thus cementing a long-standing relationship with Eastwood. (It seems typical of Eastwood that he sticks by old and trusted friends from way back.)

Like Siegel, Daley was also born in Chicago, though he spent most of his early years in Texas and California where his father acted as supervisor of a hotel chain. He attended UCLA where he studied business administration, with special emphasis on finance, accounting, and business law—qualifications that make him truly formidable as a production man.

Through an acquaintance, Daley got himself a job as an accountant in the production budget control department of Universal-International (as it was then known), working in association with Ziv Productions, Lucille Ball's Desilu, the Quinn Martin organization, and the Doris Day television series.

All this was in the early 1950s. At the time, Clint

Eastwood—who had left the army recently and was taking a course in business administration himself—was a member of the Universal talent stable, taking minor roles in a half-dozen pictures alongside names like Rock Hudson and Donald O'Connor. It was here that Daley and Eastwood became friends, for a while having apartments in the same building.

By 1957, Hollywood had begun to feel the pinch of television. Bob Daley was approached by Desilu Productions, which had acquired RKO Studios and other Hollywood holdings, to join the organization. When he joined Desilu, he worked under the aegis of production vice-president Argyle Nelson.

It is reported that Daley and Eastwood often had spoken about working together to produce pictures in what they regarded as a streamlined manner—without excessive manpower and equipment, budgeted to come in under the allocated expenditure through careful planning at the pre-production stage, and employing economy of scheduling.

It is these particular talents that Daley has brought to the Malpaso Company operation.

## Sonia Chernus

Sonia Chernus is a vivacious, hard-working woman who has spent a couple of decades or more in the film industry and who now works as story editor for the Malpaso Company.

She is a native of Los Angeles and graduated from UCLA. For several years she worked as a story editor on the CBS "Rawhide" series. She also created her own television show, "Mr. Ed." She met Clint and his wife

Maggie long before Clint Eastwood became a box-office personality, and it was Sonia Chernus who was instrumental in introducing Eastwood to Robert Sparks and Charles Marquis Warren—which, in turn, led to his long-standing engagement in the "Rawhide" television series.

Sonia Chernus now spends her time seeking out and studying books and other material that can possibly be turned into future films for the Malpaso Company. Manuscripts, books, and scripts are stacked high in her office at Universal Studios, and occasionally she ventures on buying forays to New York and London publishing houses in search of possible film material.

# 11

# Clint Eastwood
# on Directing

"WE were shooting the first sequences of
*Play Misty for Me* in the Sardine Factory at Monterey.
Don Siegel was behind the bar preparing for his role as
bartender in the opening scenes. I noticed that he looked
a little uptight—and he admitted he was nervous because
he had never acted before.

" 'That's funny,' I said, 'I don't feel at all nervous, and
I've never directed before. . . .'

"Actually it was not a nervous moment for me. It was
an exciting prospect, directing a picture for the first time.
But of course I had apprehensions too. I was concerned
about *time*, since we had a limited schedule. And I was
anxious to get the best possible production values in the
four and a half weeks we had.

"I was also somewhat apprehensive about directing
myself.

109

"One of the most difficult problems for a director appearing in his own story is to separate the character in the story from the man behind the camera. It took constant and conscious effort to be Dave Garland, the protagonist of *Misty*, at one moment and Clint Eastwood, the director of *Misty*, immediately afterwards.

"Don Siegel had tipped me that one of the first problems of the actor/director is that he may tend to slough himself off in order to favor the other actors. Generosity is admirable, but not when it is at the expense of the story.

"I found I did indeed have a tendency to neglect reaction shots and closeups of myself during the first week. But thanks to the alertness of the script supervisor, the producer, and the cinematographer, we covered this problem.

"The use of a television replay system was a terrific help in judging my own work as an actor during the filming. I feel it is indispensable for a director who is directing himself, and it is the only way to obtain an impartial view of his portrayal.

"The routine goes something like this: You line up the shot with the camera; you rehearse with the other actors; then you shoot the scene. Finally you run down the block to the sound truck and look at the scene you have just shot on the replay system.

"I have also come to learn that the most vital necessity for a director—whether or not he is directing himself—is *organization*. In fact, two kinds of organization. Obviously directing is a demanding task that requires both mental and creative organization on the director's part— he has to know what he is doing and what he intends to do.

"But even more important is the other kind of organization: the organization made up of the people who work with him. In this respect, I was particularly fortunate. I feel that our production company, Malpaso, is vigorous and growing because of the enthusiasm, dedication, and qualifications of the people who make up Malpaso.

"Starting from the top, there is Bob Daley who has been either producer or executive producer on most of the films that Malpaso has shot. He has been producer on all three films I directed (*Play Misty for Me*, *High Plains Drifter*, *Breezy*) and I mean producer in the active sense.

"A creative producer can relieve a director of an enormous load of details and follow-through, as well as making important decisions on casting, locations, and other production problems. Of course, however, once the camera starts rolling, the director is on his own.

"The function of the producer was particularly apparent on my first directorial assignment.

"When I stress the importance of an organization, I do not mean to imply that the old concept of dozens of people hanging around assists the director. On the contrary, when I went into directing I brought to it the philosophy that a director needs a lean, creative, hand-picked crew—large enough to do the job but small enough so that everyone has a sense of participation and constant involvement.

"It is the fact that we have had this kind of crew on all the films I have directed that makes it possible to come in ahead of schedule and under budget.

"With the exception of a few "epic" types of film, pictures can be made just as cheaply in America as in Europe. It is true that labor and other costs are less abroad than they are in the United States. But after years of working in all parts of Europe and Mexico, I have learned how much faster and more efficient American crews are.

"A motion picture that would take ten weeks to shoot abroad can be done easily inside the United States in six! So there is real saving on budgets by the time the film gets in the can. And there is such a variety of backgrounds in the United States that many pictures shot abroad could easily be done in America; although I agree that for the sake of authenticity there are some films that should be shot overseas.

"In the case of *Play Misty for Me* we had the advantage of not only having an excellent cast and crew—Jessica Walter's great performance as Evelyn Draper was greatly responsible for what success the film had—but we also had the added plus of my knowing the Carmel and Monterey areas like my own backyard: largely because my own backyard is right there.

"Jo Heims's script of *Play Misty for Me* appealed to me for several reasons. It was a small story that lent itself perfectly to being shot on natural sets. Working in realistic, authentic backgrounds in Europe during my years there as an actor taught me the value of utilizing such locations. The story had great entertainment values. In addition to the psychotic, horror element, it made a nice comment on the relationships of individuals to each other and the misinterpretation of commitment.

"I felt that all types of audiences could identify with the characters. And the film could be made for a reasonable budget. When I added all these factors together, it seemed ideal for a first project as a director.

"Because of prior acting commitments, I had only six weeks to prepare for *Misty*. But as every director knows, the actual preparation time is hard to estimate, since the creative process goes on in the mind for months, sometimes years, before the physical preparation begins.

"I really did not know how difficult it had been to wear both hats until I directed *Breezy*, in which I did not also appear. Not having to suit up and jump in front of the camera did give me some extra time.

"Another of the lessons I learned—and I learned it very quickly—during the shooting of *Misty* was that by keeping everyone involved in what you, the director, are doing, crews will work twice as hard and develop a tremendous *esprit de corps*. If you explain what effect you are striving for instead of saying merely, 'Put that case over there,' or, 'Set up that lamp down there,' your crew will become totally involved.

"All of them were extremely professional. I had the distinct impression at first that they were all waiting for me to prove myself as a director. But that lasted exactly one day. By the second morning we were all working together as a totally involved, compatible unit.

"My second lesson was to be carefully prepared and well organized, but yet remain flexible, so that we could move from set to set easily and without strain.

"My biggest surprise during the filming of *Misty* was when I discovered that Universal was giving me complete freedom on the production of the film—a situation which I deeply appreciated.

"*Misty* was budgeted at $950,000. We brought it in four days ahead of schedule [i.e. the film was shot inside a month—*Author*] and $50,000 under budget.

"I think this reflected the fact that we were taking the new approach to movie making. It is no longer a ride that everyone goes along for. It is a serious job, one that can be fun, but nonetheless a job seriously dedicated to making a profit. That means bringing the film in for a reasonable price—and the only reasonable price is the lowest possible cost consistent with telling your story well.

"The twenty-week schedule seems to me to be an anomaly today. It is saddling a dinosaur. I think people in the industry are aware of this. Hollywood is in no present danger of becoming the La Brea Tar Pits.

"I brought this philosophy to the entirely different set of challenges we faced on *High Plains Drifter*, which I also directed and starred in. It had the longest schedule of any film I have directed so far. We selected a highly photogenic area for the location—Mono Lake, in the Sierras.

"The brilliant colors of the backgrounds and the constantly changing cloud formations gave us the opportunity to get some very effective shots. We had to build an entire town on the shores of the lake, which had to be destroyed at the end of the film. This meant we had to shoot in continuity—and therefore we had to keep the cast on salary longer than on the average film.

"The continuity filming worked to our advantage because the editing of the film was speeded up considerably.

"Even with all this and the special effects needed throughout the picture we managed to get under the wire of our six-week schedule with two days to spare.

"Again this reflected the involvement, flexibility, and mobility of the crew and the new approach to film making.

"I must confess here that I cannot stand long locations

or productions schedules. Once you get moving, I don't see any reason to drag your feet. During production I can function more fully and efficiently if I move at full blast. Maybe it is because I am basically lazy. For me there is no happy medium.

"In post-production, I learned the lesson of patience: going over film endlessly, for hours at a time. Most cutting rooms are abysmally depressing, for no reason that I can figure out. Few of them have windows or any relief from grey walls and racks of film cans.

"I have since discovered that if we set up cutting rooms with a little atmosphere, even if it consists of only one window, then everyone's creativity—the editor, the director, everyone involved—is heightened and therefore the work is speeded up. Why be depressed if you, don't have to?

"On *High Plains Drifter* we did much of the editing on location in a log cabin, with a great view of pine trees, snow covered mountains, and bright skies. We cut *Breezy* in a small vacant office above the Hog's Breath Inn in Carmel—a restaurant of which I happen to be part owner.

"I have found since the first film that I prefer editing on the location as the picture is being shot, though I realize that it is impossible to edit the total film that way. But it does give you enough of a head start so that it cuts down on post-production time.

"Directing films has always interested me. During my eight and a half years on 'Rawhide,' I worked with many fine directors. Unconsciously I must have absorbed some knowledge from them. Then we had a few who did not do such good work; and an actor can't help but observe and think how differently he would do the same scenes if he were in the spot.

"Gradually I eased into directing by heading the second units on segments of the pictures I appeared in. Even after *Misty* I directed the jumper sequence of *Dirty Harry* one night, when Don Siegel was ill.

"I have never been what you might term a fan or cultist of specific directors, but I have admired many of them individually for specific films: William Wellman for his classic *Ox Bow Incident*, Gillo Pontecorvo for *Battle of Algiers*, and Akiro Kurosawa for *Seven Samurai* and *Red Beard*.

"But there are others, many others, and each one is distinguished for a definite and individual contribution to film making.

"I think I have learned most about film directing from working with Don Siegel, whom I respect very much as a director. His special qualities include the organized way in which he prepares for production and his economy in shooting. I do not mean dollars-and-cents economy— although it amounts to that—but his sure knowledge of what he is doing and of the shots he wants to put down on film. And not merely shooting massive footage, nine-tenths of which will be thrown away. This really boils down to editing while shooting.

"It seems to me that in the past accolades have been bestowed unfairly primarily on the motion picture directors who have spent the most time and the most money on their pictures. There are all too many directors, like Don Siegel, who were never given deserved credit for the high-quality films they turned out with extremely low budgets. Fortunately, in Don Siegel's case, this has been rectified in recent years.

"I love acting and intend to continue doing it. But I must admit that the satisfaction of directing goes deeper than in any other facet of film making. In direction, you are responsible for the entire concept of the telling of a story; in acting, you are mainly concerned with your own interpretation of one of the characters in the plot.

"But I suppose that my involvement goes even deeper than acting or directing. I love every aspect of the creation of a motion picture and I guess I am committed to it for life."

Reprinted by permission from *Action* magazine

# 12

# A Personal and Professional Assessment of Clint Eastwood

"People who go to movies like me. I have never had any promotion or big studio build-up. I have never had any picture taken kissing my dog as I get off a plane or any of that shit. There are stars who are produced by the press—I am not one of them."

"Any actor going into pictures has to have something special—that's what makes a star—while a lot of damned good actors are passed by. The public goes to see the stars. I didn't invent the rules, it's just the way it is."

We have noted that in the twenty-five or more years of Clint Eastwood's film career he has come in for more than a fair share of criticism. It is probably true to say that he is the sort of person with whom it is easy to enjoy a love-hate relationship. The Hollywood trade press has never been particularly kind to him. Some people would argue that it has pursued what amounts to a personal vendetta against him, singling out certain reporters and film reviewers by name. Why—if this is the case—should it be so?

Perhaps part of the explanation is that Clint Eastwood is very much a non-Hollywood type of person. Although he maintains his original home, purchased during the early days of success in "Rawhide," as well as a modest enough establishment in the Sherman Oaks area of the San Fernando Valley (I have seen grander homes owned by studio executives), he prefers to withdraw some 400 miles to Pebble Beach where he is establishing his permanent home base.

He has been quoted as saying that he would "go mad in a fancy house" and "it wouldn't suit Maggie either," and arguing that with travel being as easy as it is he can settle down more or less anywhere he chooses. He seems to prefer the more relaxed atmosphere of the Carmel-Monterey Peninsula area, and although the Eastwoods are surrounded by extremely wealthy neighbors, they tend to keep to themselves. In fact, Clint is more often seen in jeans and a T-shirt driving an ancient Chevrolet pickup than in a business suit boarding an airplane.

He is certainly not antisocial, though he is a shy person; he simply seems to prefer to live this way, with a genuine liking for solitude, occasionally even excluding his wife Maggie.

"Clint is definitely a loner," Maggie once explained. "He holds so much back."

"I am really just a backwoods type," Clint once said, as if in agreement. "And when I get really uptight, I go up to the house in Carmel alone, or Maggie may go on ahead of me. It depends on how we both feel."

This liking for solitude was noted by his costar Jean Seberg during the filming of *Paint Your Wagon*: "People cannot get close to Clint. He is not buddy-buddy. Every moment he had to himself out in Oregon, he was off alone . . . jogging in the woods, or in his trailer, or on a motorcycle. I think he genuinely likes solitude."

During the making of *Wagon*, Eastwood rented a farmhouse near the small town of Baker and often got up at 4:30 in the morning to tend to the animals or simply to watch the sunrise.

"He really is somebody who has his knapsack at the foot of the bed," Miss Seberg goes on. "You always have the feeling that Clint is ready to hit the road."

Talking to Tim Chadwick in *Screen Stars*, Eastwood described his attitude this way: "Some people have a need to discuss deep, intimate things about themselves, discuss and analyze. I don't feel that need. Maybe it's a strength, maybe it's a weakness. Once I went to a psychiatrist. I did it as a favor to someone who was having a problem; and after we'd talked, the guy said to me, 'You seem to have things in hand.' I think I do."

As if to demonstrate this stability, the Eastwoods will celebrate their *twentieth* wedding anniversary in November, 1974.

"Being married to the same chick for twenty years doesn't seem to be what people want—a bit of a drag," Clint once commented drily. Unlike many marriages, stability was not gained by having children; in fact, the couple waited some fourteen years before having their first child, Kyle Clinton. They also have a daughter Allison, who was born in May, 1972. The household is shared with an assortment of pets, including Sidney the basset hound, Sam the Siamese cat, and two tortoises, Fred and Francine.

It would be wrong, however, to give the impression that the Eastwoods live the lives of hermits. When entertaining, they are the perfect hosts (Maggie has often been dubbed "Miss Elegance" by columnists and others). One of the major events in the Southern California social calendar is the Eastwoods' annual tennis tournament, held at Pebble Beach, that attracts an impressive array of stars as entrants. The proceeds go to favorite charities.

When called upon, Clint Eastwood can acquit himself well in public. He does not seem overly fond of promotional tours associated with his films, finding them more tiring than acting or directing. But he is a professional and apparently accepts the need to make these tours. In April, 1973, he probably surprised a few people in the close-knit Hollywood showbiz community when he hosted the annual Academy Awards show, taking over at short notice in place of Charlton Heston who arrived late because of a flat tire.

Perhaps Eastwood is one of the industry's unsung heroes—I could not help noticing while dining amidst a glitter of illuminated panels showing colored portraits of film stars in the executive dining room at Universal Studios that their money spinner's image did not appear.

Surely, Clint Eastwood's professionalism is no more clearly indicated than in his attitude to films in general and, in particular, to his work as a director. He is passionately involved with anything to do with films and occasionally writes intelligent and coherent pieces about the problems of the industry. He is also surprisingly knowledgeable about the technical aspects of filming, and is happy to chat about lip syncs and lap dissolves with the best of them.

As a director he has been described as a pleasant person to work with, although demanding.

"I had forgotten what it was to make a picture this agreeably," said William Holden after the filming of *Breezy*. "I'll work with Clint anytime he asks. Besides, he can't pull any crap on me because he is an actor too! He's also even-tempered, a personality trait not much in evidence among directors. The crew is totally behind him and that really helps things go smoothly. There's been no temperament, nothing. We all do our own work and like it."

This transition from actor to film director is not easy. Some actors made the move easily enough—John Wayne, Peter Lawford, Robert Culp, Paul Newman, Sidney Poitier, Jack Lemmon. Others have tried once and not succeeded—Marlon Brando, Frank Sinatra, Burt Lancaster, James Cagney.

"I think it is a logical place for an actor to go," Eastwood once explained, "unless he is content to sit in his trailer between takes and do nothing else. I was never satisfied to do that. I was always an activist. I like the picture business, and I have a great curiosity about films."

One can question the sameness in Clint Eastwood's films—certainly those in which he has appeared as an actor—yet he is obviously aware that being a slave to trends can be dangerous.

Writing in the *Los Angeles Times* (August 24, 1970), he said: "It seems that each film 'makes' its own specific audience. There's an *Airport* audience and an *Easy Rider* audience . . . But the *Easy Rider* audience is not necessarily going to buy all bike films . . . Fads aren't insurance. . . . The nitty-gritty comes in seeing films at the neighborhood theaters . . . where people sometimes talk back to the actors."

Analyzing Eastwood's screen personality is a little more complicated. As he himself points out, audiences like him, and his films certainly have made money. By 1971, his films had grossed over $200,000,000, and he was commanding a salary of around $1,000,000 per picture.

Not many actors have made the transition from television hero to feature film actor successfully. Steve McQueen did. Ty Hardin had a qualified success in Europe following a long run in "Bronco." Ed Byrnes, who played the character Kookie in "77 Sunset Strip," settled in Rome and reportedly takes home $100,000 per picture.

Certainly Eastwood has, or at least has acquired, a formidable screen persona—an image completely divorced from the man inside. Or is it?

Film critic Joyce Haber writes: "Clint Eastwood has control but little ego. I have never seen him arrogant at parties with really big stars. . . . This lack of presumption, this seeming concern with others are Eastwood's style, his qualities, even more than his special charisma that will keep him on top."

And *Life* magazine (July 23, 1971) had this to say about him: "The character he plays is invariably a man in total control, able to handle anything. He is his own law and his own morality—independent, unfettered, invulnerable, unfathomable, unbelievable. He is a heavy dude. . . . His audiences are largely male and his films play well to black audiences in Harlem and Chicago."

"Eastwood does not act," wrote another critic, "but it is irrelevant. All he has to do is to stand there and look scruffy and intense and people love it. What Eastwood does have is presence. When he is on screen he is definitely, unarguably there."

Not everyone would agree entirely with these statements. Other commentators, usually male, tend to put him down. Television personality Dick Cavett has referred to Eastwood as "that cowboy star," though surprisingly columnist Rex Reed has said some nice things about him. But yet another reviewer put it this way: "An Eastwood character is a man with no soul . . . as empty inside as a bombed-out building . . . a frigid symbol of virility." When this was read to Eastwood at the time, he commented that reviewers "feel they have to find something new and clever to say. It sounds good, and I suspect they don't often know precisely what they mean."

Personally, I do not think it is all that simple. One of the paradoxes I find in examining Clint Eastwood's film career is that he appears to say one thing and do another. I refer to his professed hatred of violence in all its forms, and yet he plays violent roles in *Dirty Harry* and *High*

*Plains Drifter*. I would like to see him shift away from the conservative, play-it-safe type of film and inject his money and undoubted talents into something a little less escapist, a little more worthwhile. (It is interesting to reflect that I prepared these notes during the week that saw the American release of *The Paper Chase* and *Mean Streets*, as if to reinforce my arguments.)

Undeniably, Clint Eastwood is popular at the box office. A 1972 poll showed him to be number one star in the United States, ahead of George C. Scott, Gene Hackman, John Wayne, Barbara Streisand, Marlon Brando, Paul Newman, Steve McQueen, Dustin Hoffmann, and Goldie Hawn. But as Eastwood himself points out, there is no longer a movie audience but an audience for each film. To stay on top, I hope he will start to flex his creative muscles, as he did so well in *Breezy*.

In August, 1972, Clint Eastwood was elected to the National Council of the Arts by President Nixon. I hope he will now use his influence to help bring about an all-round upgrading of films and, in particular, an end to excessive screen violence.

# Filmography

**Revenge of the Creature** (Universal-International)    1954

Director: Jack Arnold
Screenplay: Martin Berkeley
Story: William Alland
Director of photography: Charles Wellbourne

Eastwood played the part of Jennings. Others in the cast included Brett Halsey, John Agar, John Bromfield.


**Francis in the Navy** (Universal-International)    1954

Director: Arthur Lubin
Screenplay: Devery Freeman
Director of photography: Carl Guthrie

Created by David Stern, and featuring Donald O'Connor,

playing a dual role; also starring Martha Hyer, Jim Backus, David Janssen, Paul Burke, and Chill Wills as the voice of the donkey. Eastwood played the part of Jonesey, a young sailor.

**Lady Godiva** (Universal-International)    1954

Director: Arthur Lubin
Screenplay: Oscar Brodney and Harry Ruskin
From a story by Oscar Brodney
Director of photography: Carl Guthrie

The cast included some famous names, among them Maureen O'Hara, George Nader, Victor McLaglen, Rex Reason and others. Eastwood played "the first Saxon."

**Tarantula** (Universal-International)    1954

Director: Jack Arnold
Screenplay: Robert Fresco and Martin Berkeley
From a story by Robert Fresco and Jack Arnold
Director of photography: George Robinson

Eastwood played the first pilot. Others in the cast were Raymond Bailey, John Agar, and Ed Rand.

**Never Say Good-Bye** (Universal-International)    1955

Director: Jerry Hopper
Screenplay: Charles Hoffman
Director of photography: Maury Gertsman

The film starred Rock Hudson, George Sanders, Ray Collins, David Janssen, Shelley Fabares. Eastwood played the part of Will.

**The First Traveling Saleslady (RKO Pictures)    1955**

Producer and director: Arthur Lubin
Screenplay: Devery Freeman and Stephen Longstreet
Director of photography: William Snyder

Eastwood played the part of Jack Rice—Carol Channing's beau—and the name cast included Ginger Rogers, Barry Nelson, James Arness, and Lane Chandler.

**Star in the Dust (Universal-International)    1955**

Director: Charles Haas
Screenplay: Oscar Brodney
Director of photography: John L. Russell

Eastwood played a minor part as a ranch-hand, with John Agar, Mamie Van Doren, Richard Boone, James Gleason, and Randy Stuart among the cast.

**Escapade in Japan (RKO Pictures for Universal-International release)    1956**

Director: Arthur Lubin
Screenplay: Winston Miller
Director of photography: William Snyder

Eastwood played the part of Dumbo, an air force pilot. The film also starred Teresa Wright and Cameron Mitchell.

**Ambush at Cimarron Pass (Produced by Regal for Twentieth Century-Fox.)    1957**

Director: Jodie Copelan
Screenplay: Richard Taylor and John Butler

From a story by Robert Reeds and Robert Woods
Director of photography: John M. Nicholaus, Jr.

Eastwood played the part of Keith Williams, and the cast
included Scott Brady, William Vaughan, Keith Richards, Dirk
London, and Frank Gerstle.

**Lafayette Escadrille** (Warner Brothers)    1958

Director: William A. Wellman
Screenplay: A. S. Fleischman
From a story by William W. Wellman
Director of photography: William Clothier
Assistant director: George Vieira

### Cast

| | |
|---|---|
| Thad Walker | Tab Hunter |
| Renee | Etchika Choureau |
| Drillmaster | Marcel Dalio |
| Duke Sinclaire | David Janssen |
| U.S. General | Paul Fix |
| The Madam | Veola Vann |
| Dave Putnam | Will Hutchins |
| George Moseley | Clint Eastwood |
| Dave Judd | Bob Hover |
| Arthur Bluthenthal | Tom Laughlin |
| Frank Baylies | Brett Halsey |
| Jimmy | Henry Nakamura |
| Sergeant Parris | Maurice Marsac |
| Mr. Walker | Raymond Bailey |
| Concierge | George Nardelli |
| Bill Wellman | Bill Wellman, Jr. |
| Tom Hitchcock | Jody McCrea |
| Red Scanlon | Dennis Devine |

**A Fistful of Dollars** [A co-production Jolly Film (Rome),
Constantin Film (Munich), Ocean Film (Madrid)]    1964

Producer: Harry Colombo and George Papi
Director: Sergio Leone
Director of photography: Jack Dalmas
Assistant Director: Frank Prestland

### Cast

| | |
|---|---|
| Man with No Name | Clint Eastwood |
| Marisol | Marianne Koch |
| Ramon Rojo | John Wels |
| John Baxter | W. Lukschy |
| Esteban Rojo | S. Rupp |
| Benito Rojo | Antonio Prieto |
| Silvanito | Jose Calvo |
| Consuela Baxter | Margherita Lozano |
| Julian | Daniel Martin |
| Rubio | Benny Reeves |
| Chico | Richard Stuyvesant |

**For a Few Dollars More** [A co-production PEA (Rome),
Arturo Gonzales (Madrid), Constantin Film (Munich)]
1965

Producer: Alberto Grimaldi
Director: Sergio Leone
Screenplay and dialogue: Luciano Vincenzoni
From a story by Leone and Fulvio Morzella
Director of photography: Massimo Dallamano

### Cast

| | |
|---|---|
| Man with No Name | Clint Eastwood |
| Colonel Mortimer | Lee Van Cleef |
| Indio | Gian Maria Volonte |

| | |
|---|---|
| Old man over railway | Josef Egger |
| Colonel's sister | Rosemary Dexter |
| Hotel manager's wife | Mara Krup |
| Indio's gang: | |
| The hunchback | Klaus Kinski |
| First man | Mario Brega |
| Second man | Aldo Sambrel |
| Third man | Luigi Pistilli |
| Fourth man | Benito Stefanelli |

**The Good, the Bad and the Ugly** [PEA (Rome), released through United Artists]     1966

Producer: Alberto Grimaldi
Director: Sergio Leone
Screenplay: Age-Scarpelli, Luciano Vincenzoni, and Sergio Leone
From a story by Age-Scarpelli, Luciano Vincenzoni, and Sergio Leone
Director of photography: Tonio Del Colli

### Cast

| | |
|---|---|
| The Man with No Name | Clint Eastwood |
| Tuco | Eli Wallach |
| Setenza | Lee Van Cleef |
| Aldo Giuffre | Claudio Scarchilli |
| Mario Brega | Livio Lorenzon |
| Luigi Pistilli | Antonio Castale |
| Rada Rassimov | Sandro Scarchilli |
| Enzo Petito | Benito Stefanelli |

**The Witches** (Le Streghe)    1967

Director: Vittorio de Sica
Screenplay: Cesare Zavattini, Fabio Carpi, Enzio Muzil
Director of photography: Giuseppe Macari, Giuseppe
  Rotunno

### Cast

| | |
|---|---|
| Giovanna | Silvana Mangano |
| Her husband | Clint Eastwood |
| Diabolique | Gianno Gori |
| Mandrake | Paolo Gozina |
| Gordon | Angelo Santi |
| Man at stadium | Valentino Macchi |

**Hang 'Em High** (A co-production of Leonard Freeman Productions and the Malpaso Company)    1968

Producer: Leonard Freeman
Director: Ted Post
Screenplay: Leonard Freeman and Mel Goldberg
Cinematographer: Lennie South

### Cast

| | |
|---|---|
| Jed Cooper | Clint Eastwood |
| Rachel | Inger Stevens |
| Captain Wilson | Ed Begley |
| Judge Adam Fenton | Pat Hingle |
| Jennifer | Arlene Golonka |

**Coogan's Bluff** (Universal)    1968

Producer: Don Siegel
Executive producer: Richard E. Lyons
Associate producer: Irving Leonard
Director: Don Siegel
Assistant director: Joe Cavalier
Screenplay: Herman Miller, Dean Riesner, and Howard
  Rodman
From a story by Herman Miller
Director of photography: Bud Thackery

### Cast

| | |
|---|---|
| Coogan | Clint Eastwood |
| Sergeant McElroy | Lee J. Cobb |
| Julie | Susan Clark |
| Linny Raven | Tisha Sterling |
| Ringerman | Don Stroud |
| Mrs. Ringerman | Betty Field |
| Sheriff McCrea | Tom Tully |
| Millie | Melodie Johnson |
| Jackson | James Edwards |
| Running Bear | Rudy Diaz |

**Where Eagles Dare** (A Winkast Production for MGM)
  1969

Producer: Elliott Gershwin and Jerry Kastner
Associate producers: Dennis Holt, Richard McWhorter
Director: Brian G. Hutton
Cameraman: Arthur Ibbetson
Screenplay: Alistair MacLean
Assistant directors: Colin Brewer, Patrick Clayton, Ben
  Harrison, and Chris Kenny

### Cast

| | |
|---|---|
| John Smith | Richard Burton |
| Lieutenant Schaffer | Clint Eastwood |
| Mary Ellison | Mary Ure |
| Vice-Admiral Rolland | Michael Hordern |
| Colonel Wyatt Turner | Patrick Wymark |
| Dwight Jones | Robert Beatty |
| Colonel Kramer | Anton Diffring |
| Christiansen | Donald Houston |
| Rosemeyer | Ferdy Maine |
| Laurence-Smythe | Neil McCarthy |
| Caraciola | Peter Barkworth |
| Lee Thomas | William Squire |
| Sergeant Harrard | Brook Williams |
| Colonel Weisner | Victor Beaumont |
| Heide | Ingrid Pitt |
| Von Hangen | Derren Nesbit |

**Paint Your Wagon** (Lerner-Malpaso-Paramount Production) 1969

Producer: Alan Jay Lerner
Associate producer: Tom Shaw
Director: Joshua Logan
Screenplay and lyrics: Alan Jay Lerner
Adaptation: Paddy Chayefsky
Music: Frederick Loewe
Music for additional songs: Andre Previn
Based on the musical *Paint Your Wagon* presented on stage by
    Cheryl Crawford
Director of photography: William A. Fraker

### Cast

| | |
|---|---|
| Ben Rumson | Lee Marvin |
| Pardner | Clint Eastwood |
| Elizabeth | Jean Seberg |
| Rotten Luck Willie | Harv Presnell |
| Mad Jack Duncan | Ray Walston |
| Horton Fenty | Tom Ligon |
| Parson | Alan Dexter |
| Horace Tabor | William O'Connell |
| Haywood Holbrook | Ben Baker |
| Mr. Fenty | Alan Baxter |
| Mrs. Fenty | Paula Trueman |
| Atwell | Robert Easton |
| Foster | Geoffrey Norman |
| Jacob Woodling | John Mitchum |

## Kelly's Heroes (Production Katz/Loeb/MGM)    1970

Director: Brian G. Hutton
Assistant director: John C. Chulay
Screenplay: Troy Kennedy Martin
Cameraman: Gabriel Figueroa

### Cast

| | |
|---|---|
| Kelly | Clint Eastwood |
| Big Joe | Telly Savalas |
| Crapgame | Don Rickles |
| General Colt | Carroll O'Connor |
| Oddball | Donald Sutherland |
| Moriarty | Gavin McLeod |
| Maitland | Hal Buckley |
| Little Joe | Stuart Margolin |
| Cowboy | Jeff Morris |
| Gutowsky | Richard Davos |

**Two Mules for Sister Sara** (Martin Rackin Productions/
   Universal)     1970

Director: Don Siegel
Assistant directors: Joe Cavalier and Manuel Munoz
Screenplay: Albert Maltz
From a story by Bud Boettichar
Cameraman: Gabriel Figueroa

### Cast

| | |
|---|---|
| Sara | Shirley MacLaine |
| Hogan | Clint Eastwood |
| Colonel Beltran | Manolo Fabregas |
| General Leclair | Alberto Morin |
| First American | Armando Silvestre |
| Second American | John Kelly |
| Third American | Enrique Lucero |
| Juan | David Estuardo |
| Juan's mother | Aida Carasco |
| Juan's father | Pancho Cordoba |
| Horacio | Jose Cervez |

**Play Misty for Me** (A Malpaso Company Production)     1971

Producer: Robert Daley
Associate producer: Bob Larson
Director: Clint Eastwood
Screenplay: Jo Heims and Dean Riesner
From a story by Jo Heims
Director of photography: Bruce Surtees
"Misty" composed and performed by Erroll Garner
"The First Time Ever I Saw Your Face" sung by Roberta Flack

### Cast

| | |
|---|---|
| Dave Garver | Clint Eastwood |
| Evelyn Draper | Jessica Walters |

| Tobie | Donna Mills |
| Sergeant McCallum | John Larch |
| Frank | Jack Ging |
| Madge | Irene Hervey |
| Al Monte | James McEachin |
| Birdie | Clarice Taylor |
| Murphy | Don Siegel |
| Jay Jay | Duke Everts |

## Dirty Harry (A Malpaso Company Production)    1971

Producer and director: Don Siegel
Executive producer: Robert Daley
Associate producer: Carl Pingitore
Assistant director: Robert Rubin
Screenplay: Harry Julian Fink, R. M. Fink, and Dean Riesner
Director of photography: Bruce Surtees

### Cast

| Harry Callahan | Clint Eastwood |
| Bressler | Harry Guardino |
| Chico | Reni Santoni |
| Killer | Andy Robinson |
| Chief | John Larch |
| DeGeorgio | John Mitchum |
| Mrs. Russell | Mae Mercer |
| Norma | Lyn Edgington |
| Bus driver | Ruth Kobart |
| Mr. Jaffe | Woodrow Parfrey |
| Rothko | Josef Sommer |
| Bannerman | William Paterson |
| Liquor proprietor | James Nolan |
| Sid Kleinman | Maurice S. Argent |

| Miss Willis | Jo de Winter |
| Sergeant Reineke | Craig G. Kelly |
| The Mayor | John Vernon |

## The Beguiled (Universal/Malpaso Company)     1971

Producer and director: Don Siegel
Associate producer: Claude Traverse
Screenplay: John B. Sherry and Grimes Grice
From the novel by Thomas Cullinan
Director of photography: Bruce Surtees
Assistant director: Burt Astor

### Cast

| John McBurney | Clint Eastwood |
| Martha Farnsworth | Geraldine Page |
| Edwina Dabney | Elizabeth Hartman |
| Carol | Jo Ann Harris |
| Doris | Darleen Carr |
| Hallie | Mae Mercer |
| Amy | Pamelyn Ferdin |
| Abigail | Melody Thomas |
| Lizzie | Peggy Drier |
| Janie | Pattye Mattick |

## Joe Kidd (Universal/Malpaso Company)     1972

Producer: Sidney Beckerman
Executive producer: Robert Daley
Director: John Sturges
Assistant director: Jim Fargo
Screenplay: Elmore Leonard
Director of photography: Bruce Surtees

### Cast

| | |
|---|---|
| Joe Kidd | Clint Eastwood |
| Frank Harlan | Robert Duvall |
| Luis Chama | John Saxon |
| Lamarr | Don Stroud |
| Helen Sanchez | Stella Garcia |
| Mingo | James Wainwright |
| Roy | Paul Koslo |
| Mitchell | Gregory Walcott |
| Hotel manager | Dick Van Patten |
| Elma | Lynne Marta |

## High Plains Drifter (Universal/Malpaso Company)    1973

Producer: Robert Daley
Executive producer: Jennings Lang
Director: Clint Eastwood
Assistant director: Jim Fargo
Screenplay: Ernest Tidyman
Director of photography: Bruce Surtees

### Cast

| | |
|---|---|
| The Stranger | Clint Eastwood |
| Sarah Belding | Verna Bloom |
| Callie Travers | Mariana Hill |
| Dave Drake | Mitchell Ryan |
| Morgan Allen | Jack Ging |
| Mayor Jason Hobart | Stefan Gierasch |
| Lewis Belding | Ted Hartley |
| Mordecai | Billy Curtis |
| Stacey Bridges | Geoffrey Lewis |
| Bill Borders | Scott Walker |
| Sheriff Sam Shaw | Walter Barnes |
| Lutie Naylor | Paul Brinegar |

| | |
|---|---|
| Asa Goodwin | Richard Bull |
| Preacher | Robert Donner |
| Bootmaker | John Hillerman |
| Cole Carlin | Anthony James |
| Barber | William O'Connell |
| Jake Ross | John Quade |
| Townswoman | Jane Aull |
| Dan Carlin | Dan Vadis |
| Gunsmith | Reid Cruickshanks |
| Tommy Morris | James Gosa |
| Saddlemaker | Jack Kosslyn |
| Fred Short | Russ McCubbin |
| Mrs. Lake | Belle Mitchell |
| Warden | John Mitchum |
| Teamster | Carl C. Pitti |
| Stableman | Chuck Waters |
| Marshall Jim Duncan | Buddy Van Horn |

**Breezy** (Universal/Malpaso Company)    1973

Producer: Robert Daley
Associate producer: Jo Heims
Executive producer: Jennings Lang
Director: Clint Eastwood
Screenplay: Jo Heims
Director of photography: Frank Stanley

### Cast

| | |
|---|---|
| Frank Harmon | William Holden |
| Breezy | Kay Lenz |
| Bob Henderson | Roger C. Carmel |
| Betty | Marj Dusay |
| Paula | Joan Hotchkis |
| Marcy | Jamie Smith Jackson |

| | |
|---|---|
| Man in car | Norman Bartold |
| Overnight date | Lynn Borden |
| Nancy | Shelly Morrison |
| Bruno | Dennis Olivieri |
| Charlie | Eugene Peterson |
| Police officer | Lew Brown |
| Doctor | Richard Bull |
| Norman | Johnnie Collins III |
| Maître d' | Don Diamond |
| Veterinarian | Scott Holden |
| Real estate agent | Sandy Kenyon |
| Driver | Jack Kosslyn |
| Waitress | Mary Munday |
| Saleswoman | Frances Stevenson |
| Paula's escort | Buck Young |
| Dress customer | Priscilla Morrill |
| Sir Love-A-Lot | Earle |

# Index

143

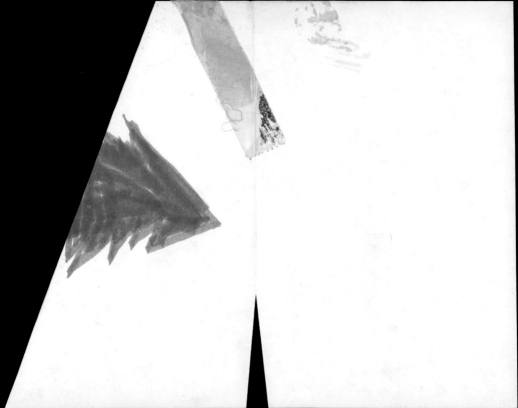

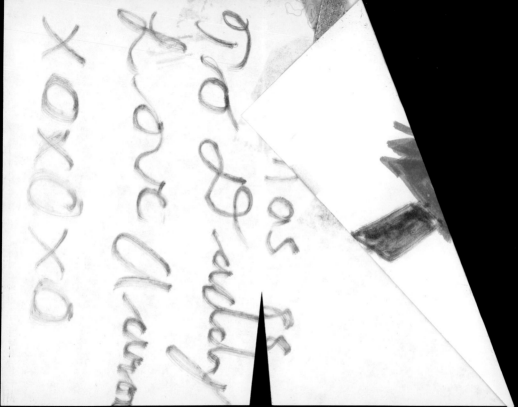

# THE WAY THEY WERE
# IN THE
# STAR ILLUSTRATED HISTORY
# OF THE MOVIES

## HUMPHREY BOGART
## KATHARINE HEPBURN
## CLARK GABLE
## BETTE DAVIS
## MARLON BRANDO
## MARILYN MONROE
## INGRID BERGMAN
## PAUL NEWMAN

**Lavishly illustrated volumes
presenting a comprehensive overview
of the all-time great stars.**

**Now available inexpensively in large
format paperback editions.**

# STAR BOOKS

are available through all good
booksellers but, where difficulty is encountered,
titles can usually be obtained *by post* from:

Star Book Service,
G.P.O. Box 29,
Douglas,
Isle of Man,
British Isles.

1 or 2 books – retail price + 5p. each copy
3 or more books – retail price post free.

Customers outside Britain should include 7p.
postage and packing for every book ordered.